Warrior • 51

OSPREY
JG

CW00348789

Russian Grena and Infantry 1799–1815

Laurence Spring • Illustrated by Bill Younghusband

First published in Great Britain in 2002 by Osprey Publishing, Elms Court, Chapel Way, Botley, Oxford OX2 9LP, United Kingdom.
Email: info@ospreypublishing.com

ISBN 1 84176 380 2

Editor: Nikolai Bogdanovic
Editorial consultant: Philip Haythornthwaite
Design: Ken Vail Graphic Design, Cambridge, UK
Index by Alan Rutter
Originated by Grasmere Digital Imaging, Leeds, UK
Printed in China through World Print Ltd.

02 03 04 05 06   10 9 8 7 6 5 4 3 2 1

FOR A CATALOGUE OF ALL BOOKS PUBLISHED BY OSPREY MILITARY AND AVIATION PLEASE CONTACT:

Osprey Direct USA, c/o MBI Publishing, PO Box 1, 729 Prospect Ave, Osceola, WI 54020, USA. Email: info@ospreydirectusa.com

Osprey Direct UK, PO Box 140, Wellingborough, Northants, NN8 2FA, United Kingdom. Email: info@ospreydirect.co.uk

www.ospreypublishing.com

Artist's note

Readers may care to note that the original paintings from which the colour plates in this book were prepared are available for private sale. All reproduction copyright whatsoever is retained by the Publishers. All enquiries should be addressed to:

Bill Younghusband,
Moorfield,
Kilcolman West,
Buttevant,
Co.Cork,
Eire

The Publishers regret that they can enter into no correspondence upon this matter.

Acknowledgements

The author would like to thank the following without whose help this book would not have been possible: the staff of the British Library; the Public Record Office; the Army Medical Museum at Keogh Barracks, Mytchett, Hampshire; the Borodino and Russian State Museums; the L'Armée Museum, Paris; the Anne K Brown University's Military Library; and the members of the Russian Army Study Group who have contributed articles for the group's newsletter over the years, especially Doug Matthews and Mark Conrad.

FRONT COVER **The Battle of Vyazma, October 22, 1812, by P. H. Hess. (Courtesy of the Russian State Museum)**

CONTENTS

RUSSIAN GRENADIERS AND INFANTRY 1799–1815

INTRODUCTION

In the 18th and 19th centuries, the backbone of the Russian Army was the peasant and serf population. A few select statistics from the Azimov Regiment clearly show how the working man shouldered the burden of military service: in 1795, 74 percent of the recruits sent to the regiment were serfs (although this decreased to 37 percent by 1811), and 24 percent were state peasants (increasing to 53 percent in 1811). The remaining two percent were either townsmen (who consisted of artisans and tradesmen), or minorities, like Tatars. Like other members of society both peasant and serf had to pay a poll tax which formed the basis of conscription, but Jews, the clergy and other members of society (such as the nobles and merchants) were exempt from military service.

The serf, or seigniorial peasant, was the lowest inhabitant in Russia, owned by a master on whose estate he lived and worked. Some richer peasants possessed one or two serfs, whereas a nobleman could own several thousand. Serfs lived in the same conditions as the peasant but had fewer rights. Born into serfdom they could be bought and sold by their masters at will; escape was by flight, granting of freedom, or death. Masters could not have a serf put to death, but they could order punishment, such as being beaten with rods – and several cases of this are known to have resulted in death.

The majority of the peasant population subsisted as agricultural labourers, living in wooden cabins, called *izba,* which were meagrely furnished. Within the cabin a table, some benches and a large stove were standard. They cooked their meals on the stove during the day and at night slept on it. A religious icon was not unusual; they observed 153 Holy Days a year, mostly between November and February.

Between April and September most of the serfs spent their time sowing and harvesting crops. They were expected to work on their landlord's property before working on their own land. Paul I (1754–1801; r.1796) tried to restrict labour on a landlord's property to three days a week, but this was often ignored so peasants ended up working their land in the evenings. However, during wintertime, with the crops gathered in, the peasant had little to do.

Another way to escape was military service, although this was dreaded by most of the population. The threat of being sent to the army was enough punishment for most serfs. Pestel (a future Decembrist) wrote that the serf and peasant 'have become accustomed to regarding military service as the bitterest misfortune, almost as a definite sentence of death'.

Few officers mentioned the common soldier in their memoirs and despite the fact that many thousands of soldiers served in the Russian Army during the period under discussion, only two accounts of the private soldier during the Napoleonic Wars are known to exist; that of Pamfil Nazarov (who served in the infantry) and Ivan Minaev, who entered the cavalry. Both survived 25 years of service in the army, but for many the only outcome of military service was a grave in a distant field or country.

CHRONOLOGY

War of the Second Coalition

Tsar Paul I sent out three armies: to Switzerland under Rimski-Korsakov; Italy under Suvarrov; and to Holland, under Hermann.

1799

21 April	Suvarrov captures the town of Brescia.
29 April	Suvarrov captures Milan.
1 May	Suvarrov captures Pavia.
26 May	Suvarrov captures the town of Turin, but the castle holds out until 20 June.
8–10 June	Suvarrov defeats a French force at the Battle of Trebbia.
27 June	Siege of Alessandria (the city surrenders on 22 July).
28 July	Capture of the town of Mantua.
15 Aug	Suvarrov defeats the French at the Battle of Novi.
27 Aug–18 Sep	Anglo-Russian force under the Duke of York and General Hermann lands in the Helder.
8 Sep	Suvarrov leaves Italy to join Rimski-Korsakov's force in Switzerland.
19 Sep	Anglo-Russian Army narrowly defeats a Franco-Dutch Army at the Battle of Bergen.
25–26 Sep	The Russian Army of Rimski-Korsakov is defeated at the second Battle of Zurich.
2 Oct	Anglo-Russian Army defeats a Franco-Dutch Army at the Battle of Alkmaar (the Second Battle of Bergen) in the Helder.
6 Oct	Anglo-Russian Army defeated by a Franco-Dutch Army at the Battle of Castricum.
18 Oct	Convention of Alkmaar, Anglo-Russian forces agree to withdraw from The Netherlands.
19 Nov	Anglo-Russian Army evacuates the Helder.
Nov 1799– July 1800	The Russian Army, formerly under Hermann, quarter for the winter in the Channel Islands and some seaports in Britain.

1801

12 Jan	23,000 Cossacks are ordered to invade India.
Mar	The Russian invasion of India is cancelled after Tsar Paul I is assassinated. His son Alexander I succeeds.

1803–1813 Russo-Persian War

1804

14 Jan	The Persian fortress of Ganzha is stormed by General Tsitsianov.
1 July	General Tsitsianov defeats a Persian Army at Echmiadzinom.
5 July	Defeat of the Persian forces at the River Araks and the beginning of the siege of Erivan by General Tsitsianov (lifted on 4 September).

1805

5 July	Defeat of the Persian advance guard by Colonel Karyangin near the River Askaran.
9 July	Defeat of a Persian army by General Karyagin.
31 July	Repulse of an attack by Persian forces from the fortress of Ganzha by General Tsitsianov's army.
21 Dec	A detachment of General Tsitsianov's army captures the town of New Shemah.

1806

19 Feb	General Tsitsianov is murdered during negotiations concerning the surrender of Baku.
1 May	Skirmish between General Lisanevich's forces with those of Ibragin Khan near the town of Shushin.
19 June	Defeat of the Persian advanced guard of Abbas Mirzi near the River Hanaship.
24 June	Russians occupy Baku, which results in the temporary cessation of hostilities.

1807

May	Franco-Persian treaty. French troops arrive in Persia.

1808

9 Oct	Defeat of a Persian army at Karabahom.
16 Nov	The Russians assault and capture the town of Erivan.
13 Dec	Temporary cessation of hostilities.

1810

21 May	Russian force under Major General Nebolsin invades the Karabah's Khanate.
25 June	Russian force defeats the Ahmet Khan's force near the River Araks and storms the fortified town of Migri.
12–16 July	Ahmet Khan's forces are routed near the town of Migri.
16–17 Sep	Battle between a Russian army under Major General Pauluchoi and Hussein Kuln Khan's forces at the Battle of Ahalkalaki.
14–19 Dec	Russians storm the fortified town of Ahalkalaki. Cessation of hostilities and peace negotiations begin.

1812

23 Mar	Resumption of military hostilities.
1 April	Russians defeat the Persian advanced guard at Karabahom.
13 May	Battle of Sultan-Buda.
13 Aug	The Persian advance guard is defeated at Baku and is pursued to the River Kuroi.
30 Oct	Persian Army under Abbas Mirzi is defeated near the River Daurt-Clay.
31 Oct	Abbas Mirzi is again defeated at Landuz.

1813

2 Jan	The fortress of Arkevan surrenders to a Russian force.
6–11 Jan	The siege and storming of the fortress of Lenkoran by a Russian force. Cessation of hostilities.
23 Oct	The Peace of Gulistan ends the Russo-Persian War.

1805 War of the Third Coalition

8 Sep	The Austrian Army under General Mack invades Bavaria, France's ally, and occupies Ulm.
20 Oct	General Mack surrenders at Ulm.
26 Oct	Napoleon begins his pursuit of Kutuzov's Russian Army.
16 Nov	Prince Bagration's rear guard action at Hollabrunn against Murat enables Kutuzov's army time to retreat.
2 Dec.	The Russo-Austrian army is defeated at the Battle of Austerlitz,
26 Dec	Peace of Pressburg ends the war of the Third Coalition.

Mediterranean Sea Campaign of 1805–1807

1806

11 Mar	Russian troops land at Cattaro.
5 April	The French garrison of the Island of Kurtsal surrenders after Russian troops land on the island.
26 May	The French defeat a Russian force near Ragusa.
30 Sep–1 Oct	The French are defeated by a force of Russians, Serbians and

	Montenegrins at the Battle of Castelnuovo, who capture the town.
2 Oct	The Russians defeat a French force at the Battle of Cattaro.
22 Nov	Russian troops land on the Island of Brac and capture the French fortifications.

1807

| 3 Mar | Russian troops capture the Turkish fortifications on the Island of Imbros. |
| 21 Mar | Russians capture the Island of Tenedos. |

1806–1807 War of the Fourth Coalition

1806

| 26 Dec | Russians defeat the French at the Battle of Golymin, but are defeated at Pultusk. |

1807

25 Jan	The French defeat a Russian force at Mohrungen.
3 Feb	The French defeat a Russian force at Bergfried.
6 Feb	The French defeat a Russian force at Hof.
7–8 Feb	Bennigsen fights Napoleon to a draw at Eylau, but Napoleon claims a victory.
16 Feb	The French defeat a Russian force at Ostrolenka.
26 Feb	The French defeat a Russian force at Braunsberg.
5 June	The Russians defeat a French force at Lomitten.
5–6 June	The Russians defeat a French force at Guttstadt and Deppen.
14 June	Battle of Friedland Bennigsen won by Napoleon.
7–9 July	Treaty of Tilsit.

1806–1812 The Turkish War

1806

25 Dec	A Russian Army occupies the town of Hotina.
26 Dec	A Russian Army occupies the town of Yassi.
27 Dec	A Russian Army occupies the town of Bucharest
28 Dec	The capture of Akkermana.
29 Dec	The capture of the fortress of Kilna.

1807

9 Jan	A Russian force besieges the fortress of Izmail.
13 Mar	A Turkish force is defeated at Izmailom.
8 April	The fortress of Kilna surrenders to a Russian force.
10 June	Napoleon repulses the Russians at Heilsburg.
13 June	A Russian force under General Miloradovitch defeats a Turkish force at the Battle of Obileshtami.

1809

1 May	The Russians besiege the town of Brailov.
22 Aug	A Russian force under Bagration captures the fortress of Babadag.
31 Aug	Bagration's force captures the fortress of Girsovo.
10 Sep	A Russian force captures the fortress of Kustendzhi.
18 Sep	Bagration defeats a Turkish force at Rassevaton.
10 Oct	The Turkish garrison of Izmail surrenders after a long siege.
29 Oct	The Turkish garrison of Brailov surrenders after a long siege.

1810

31 May	A Russian force under Major General Kamenski storms the fortress of Bazardzhik.
3 June	The Russians storm Bazardzhik.
3–10 June	The Russians lay siege to and capture Silistria.
8 June	Kamenski defeats the Turkish advance guard at Varnoi.
12 June	Razgrad surrenders to a Russian force.
23/24 June	The Turks defeat a Russian force at Schumla.
2 Aug	Russians defeat a Turkish force at Taschlimechle.

| 26 Sep | Kamenski's force storms the fortress of Rushchuk. |
| 7 Sep | Kamenski defeats a Turkish force at Batinye. |

1811

11 Feb	A Russian force storms the Lovca.
4 July	General Kutuzov defeats the Vizier's army at Rushchuk.
2 Aug	The Russians defeat a Turkish force at Kalafotum.
9 Sep	The Turks defeat a Russian force at Giurgevo.
9 Oct	Kutuzov defeats the Turkish advance guard at Slobodzeei and the beginning of the blockade of the remaining Turkish Army.
6 Dec	The capitulation of the Turkish Army at Slobodzeei.
8 Dec	Giurevo surrenders to a Russian force.

1812

| 16 May | Truce signed between Russia and Turkey. |
| 22 June | Treaty of Bucharest, ending hostilities and releasing the Army of Moldavia to take part in Patriotic War. |

1808–1809 Russo-Swedish War

1808

20 Feb	Russian force invades Finland, beginning the Russo-Swedish War. Denmark supports Russia with skirmishes along its borders and by dropping propaganda leaflets from hot-air balloons. Active French aid does not materialise.
18 April	The Swedish Army defeats a Russian force at the Battle of Siikajoki.
14 July	Russian Army defeats a Swedish force at the Battle of Lappo.
14 Sep	Russian Army defeats a Swedish force at the Battle of Oravais.
27 Oct	A Russian force is defeated at the Battle of Virta Bro.

1809

Apr–Oct	Russia gives minimal support to Napoleon in his war against Austria.
19 Aug	Russian Army defeats a Swedish force at the Battle of Savar.
17 Sep	Peace of Fridrikshamn, Sweden cedes Finland and the Aland islands to Russia.

The Patriotic War of 1812

24 June	Napoleon's Grande Armée, 500,000 strong, invades Russia.
23 July	Action at Mohilev (Mogilev).
17 Aug	Battle of Smolensk, action at Polotsk.
19 Aug	Battle of Valutino.
7 Sep	Battle of Borodino is inconclusive despite heavy losses on both sides.
14 Sep	Napoleon enters Moscow.
18 Oct	The Grande Armée's retreat begins at the Battle of Vinkovo, or Taruntino.
24 Oct	Battle of Maloyaroslavets, Russians prevent Napoleon marching into southern Russia and he is forced to retreat the way he came.
16–17 Nov	Action at Krasnyi.
26–28 Nov	Grande Armée crosses the Berezina.
13 Dec	Last remnants of the Grande Armée leaves Russian soil.

1813 War of Liberation

13 Jan	Russian troops cross the River Nieman.
19 Mar	Russia and Prussia form an alliance.
2 May	Russo-Prussian Army is defeated by Napoleon at the Battle of Lutzen.
20–21 May	Russo-Prussian Army is defeated by Napoleon at the Battle of Bautzen.
4 June–16 Aug	Armistice; Austria enters the war on the Russo-Prussian side.
23 Aug	Russo-Prussian Army defeats a French army corps under Oudinot at Grossbeeren.
26–27 Aug	Battle of Dresden, French victory.
16–19 Oct	Napoleon is defeated by the allies at Leipzig.

1814

1 Jan	The Allies cross the Rhine into France.
29 Jan	Battle of Brienne.
1 Feb	The Allies narrowly gain a victory at the Battle of La Rothiere.
10–27 Feb	Russian troops involved in action at Champaubert, Montmirail, Chateau-Thierry, Vauchamps, Valjouan, Bar-sur-Aube.
7 Mar	Napoleon beats a Russian force at Craonne. The Prussian force present fails to launch an attack on the French.
20–21 Mar	The Allies gain a minor victory at the Battle of Arcis-sur-Aube.
25 Mar	Battle of La Fère-Champenoise.
26 Mar	Napoleon routs a Russian force under Winzingerode at St Dizier.
31 Mar	Alexander enters Paris.
12 Apr	Napoleon abdicates.
2–4 June	Allied troops leave Paris.

1815

2 Mar	Napoleon lands in France, Russia mobilises.
18 June	Napoleon is defeated at Waterloo.
10 July	Alexander I enters Paris.

Levy no.	Year	No. of 'souls' per 500	Age	Height (cm)	No. of recruits raised
	1799	1			
73rd	1802	2	17–35	160	63,198
74th	1803	2			63,198
75th	1804	1			31,293
76th	1805	4		158	126,392
77th	1806	4	17–36	158	157,997
	1807	*militia raised instead*			262,924
78th	1808	5	19–37	158	157,997
79th	1809	5	19–37	158	157,997
80th	1810	3	19–37	158	93,867
81st	1811	4	18–37	155.5	126,392
82nd	1812	3	18–40	151.25	589,748
83rd	1812	10	18–37	151.25	
84th	1812	7		151.25	
85th	1813	8	19–40		264,391
	1814	*no levy*			
86th	1815	2	19–35		63,198
TOTAL					**2,158,592**

Chart showing the number of recruits raised between 1802 and 1815. The heights and ages given are the official requirements for each levy. In practice these limitations were frequently ignored.

CONSCRIPTION

During August or September each year, a *Ukaz*, or decree, was issued by the Imperial authorities to the *Kazennaya palata* (the local government officer). He would set up a recruiting board with both civilian and military officials, headed by a military receiver or *voyennyy priemschchik*. The *Ukaz* was accompanied by an Imperial writ stating how many recruits were needed – usually one to eight 'souls' from a serf's district of 500 men. In 1812, three levies, equivalent to 20 souls in 500, were imposed: the country that had been overrun by the enemy was exempt from conscription but was charged at an increased rate in 1813.

Vagrants, criminals and servants (sent by their masters) were often sent to the army as punishment. The recruiting board, or *rekrutskoye prisutstviye*, would make up the levy required from the poll tax population of peasants and townspeople. Lots were drawn to see which families would supply a recruit. The family had to choose a member to become a soldier. This Hobson's choice usually fell upon the person with the least responsibility within the household. In 1811 Admiral Mordvinov reported to the Tsar that upon hearing of a new levy 'any young man will try to hide: [and] for this reason his relatives place him under guard, shackle him in irons, [and] treat him like a villain'.

The authorities were careful not to ruin a family, as they still had to work the land and pay the poll tax. A household with two or more males would be chosen in favour of a family with just one. In areas like Siberia, conscription was kept to a minimum in order not to depopulate the district. Payments could be made in lieu of recruitment or an official bribed not to choose them. Richer peasants frequently 'bought' poorer ones to take their place. This practice is known to have taken place on the Lieven estate at Baki, Kostroma province; in 1816 the inhabitants contributed between 2,000 and 10,000 roubles to buy substitutes. The price of a substitute was fixed at 360, and later 500, roubles.

Substitute conscripts advertised in newspapers like the *St Petersburg Gazette*; an advertisement in 1793 offered 'for sale as surplus, a 22 year old man, trained in women's dressmaking, who is suitable also as a recruit'. There also appears to have been a trade in substitutes; merchants bought serfs from their masters and sold them on to would-be conscripts. To reduce such abuses, merchants could only buy one serf at a time, no serf could be sold within three months of the *Ukaz* being issued, and all had to be registered.

Although families preferred their single men to enlist, this was not always possible. In *From Serf to Russian Soldier*, historian E. K. Wirtschafter notes that 50 percent of recruits sent to the Azov Infantry Regiment in 1795 were married and this rose to 56 percent in 1811. In addition there were height and age requirements for recruits; in 1766 the minimum height was 160 cm and age limits 17 to 35. In 1808 the minimum age increased to 19; then because more recruits were needed the height limit was reduced to 151 cm in 1812, and age limits were 12 to 40. (In some areas older men were sent as recruits, having outlived their usefulness on their master's estate. Prince Lieven's estate accounts record a 58-year-old peasant being conscripted.) In 1815, with the Napoleonic Wars over, the height and age limit returned to their 1766 levels.

Martha Wilmot, an Irishwoman who toured Russia with her sister and stayed in St Petersburg with Princess Daschkaw, recalls the conscription process in her journal for 12 November 1805:

'Yesterday was the melancholy day for giving up to Government the recruits which the Princess was obliged to furnish. This year there are four men taken from every 500 ... The man who goes as a soldier is considered dead to his family ... This idea arises from the size of the Empire which (together with bad posts and little notion of reading and writing among that class) makes any news from a soldier a thing scarcely if ever possible'.

A print depicting a recruit leaving his family to join the army, entitled 'Blessing of a volunteer, 1812' by A. G. Ukhtomsky. The recruit's father is presenting his son with a religious icon in the hope that it will keep him safe. Meanwhile a soldier stands at the door waiting to take him to his new life as a soldier. (Courtesy of the Russian State Museum)

Sir Robert Wilson, a British liaison officer with the Russian Army between 1807 and 1814, recorded a similar scene.

'The day of nomination is passed in general grief and each family is in unaffected affliction at the approaching separation of a son or a brother. But no sooner is the head of the reluctant conscript shaved, according to military habit; no sooner is he recognised as a defender of his country, than the plaints and lamentation cease.'

However, Robert Lyall, a contemporary of Wilson, recorded a different picture:

'I have seen the recruits upon *telegas* and sledges, drawn at a solemn pace, and surrounded by their relations and friends who bewailed their fate in the most lamentable manner; while they dejected and absorbed in grief, sat like statues or lay extended like corpses.'

Conscripts were taken to the recruiting officer; if they were found fit for service they had their foreheads and beards shaved off to identify them as recruits. Foreheads had to remain shaven for the next six months. They were also put in irons to prevent them running away. Those found unfit for service were free to return home, to the delight of their families, but this meant another serf had to be chosen. Martha Wilmot notes on 14 November 1805:

'The steward is returned this evening from Kaluga ... with seven out of ten recruits which he conducted to the army a few days ago or rather to the captain of the Guards sent from St Petersburg to accept them and reject others who did not fit the standard for height, length, breadth of chest and shoulders etc. etc. by which they were measured.'

Self-mutilation was a common way to avoid conscription; cutting off a finger or having two or three teeth missing would mean that they were unable to pull the trigger on their musket, or bite the top off a cartridge and so could not load the musket. Skin disorders, ear infections and hair loss were considered grounds for discharging a recruit from service. However, if a peasant was found to have deliberately made himself unserviceable he would be severely punished.

To prevent deliberate mutilation, the authorities decided to accept recruits who were suffering from various conditions. In 1828 recruits with mange were enlisted in the ranks and cases in the civilian population declined dramatically.

A group of soldiers being shaved. Ivan Minayev, a private soldier, wrote in his memoirs that he was 'greatly shaken when I woke up the next day, as it happened opposite a mirror, and saw myself with my [beard and] forehead shorn'. (Courtesy of Anne S. K. Brown University Library)

However, even before these reforms, bribing officials to accept an unfit recruit for service was common. G. A. Stroganov had to supply 18 recruits from his Perm estate, in 1795; bribing officials cost 460 roubles, 25 roubles went to the doctor to pass recruits as fit for duty.

A typical recruit was Pamfil Nazarov, born on 9 February 1792 in the village of Selikov: he has left one of only two accounts of a private soldier in this period. He recalls his entry into the army, agreeing to be conscripted for the sake of his married brothers and his two-year-old niece and goddaughter. He was taken to the Government building in the provincial capital Tver. Called into the building he was left standing in just a shirt until the governor asked:

' "Which one of you is Pamfil?" I, in a pitiful voice, answered "I am Pamfil." Looking at me, he gave a sign to a soldier standing behind me, who I had not noticed in order that he could remove my shirt; the shirt was taken off, which seemed to me very strange, and which caused me embarrassment and shyness, when perceiving I was surrounded by several hundred men, who turned their attention on me like a convict. The governor ordered me to be led to the doctor, who examined me in the mouth and all the exterior and asked "All is healthy?" I answered that I was healthy and the doctor reported this to the governor … The governor ordered me to be measured and me being two arshins four versks [159.6 cm]. The governor called out "forehead!" and [the shaving of my forehead] … was carried out. I was dressed in a garment and taken under guard. After this the levy was ordered to swear [an oath of allegiance to the Tsar] and afterwards delivered to our lodgings.'

This image, taken from A. V. Viskovatov's epic work on the Russian Army, shows an example of the recruit's uniform introduced on 23 May 1808. These were made of grey cloth, and were paid for by the recruits' local community. (Author's collection)

The recruit was issued with a peasant's caftan, trousers and a pair of shoes, which was to last him until he received his first uniform. From 23 May 1808 each recruit received a grey or white soldier's coat, pantaloons, a forage cap, a black cravat, a pair of lacquered boots, and a knapsack in which to put his belongings. The recruit's village paid for his uniform, travelling expenses, and 1.50 roubles per man which was issued on the journey to his regiment. Recruits were handed to an escort who divided them into *artels* (the lowest administrative unit within a regiment) of eight to ten men; members of the *artel* supported each other in the long march that followed. In theory each recruit also received six measures of flour, three pecks of croup per day and 6 pounds of salt per month.

The following day a roll call was held for the recruits and relatives said good-bye to them. 'I ran to my mother,' wrote Pamfil Nazarov. 'She caught sight of me in flood of tears … [I] persuaded my mother … that instead of crying, she say a prayer to God.' After several days this band of recruits was ordered to St Petersburg.

In 1812 to match the changes in military fashion a new uniform for recruits was issued. This picture from A. V. Viskovatov's work, shows these changes. The 27th French bulletin dated 27 October 1812 recalls that at the Battle of Maloyaroslavitz 'We found on the field 1700 Russians, amongst whom were 1100 recruits, dressed in grey jackets, having hardly served two months.' (Author's collection)

Some of the recruits' relatives could not bear to be parted from them and journeyed to St Petersburg to get one last glimpse of their sons or brothers, as Robert Ker Porter, an Englishman touring Russia at the beginning of the 19th century, recalls:

'it is with the affectionate hope of again seeing their different relatives, that many very aged men accompany these frozen caravans [to] St Petersburg … The knowledge of that city and of their village bounds their geographic acquirements, it is thither all their wishes tend; for to that spot alone, they falsely believe is fixed the subject of their fond solicitude. Ignorant of any particular corps, and only conscious that it is a *soldier* they seek … they momentarily look for the blessing of again embracing a son, a brother, or some other near and beloved kinsman. Actuated by similar feelings, hundreds of soldiers (after their military duties are over for the day) are seen going from group to group, searching for their own parents amongst these patriarchal strangers … the heart saddens while listening to the impatient enquiries of many who are soon deprived of their dearest hopes, by the information that another country contains their offspring, perhaps another world.'

There were some bonuses to enlistment: except on campaign, the recruit would be fed regularly and new uniforms were issued every year. The wives and children of married recruits were also freed from their landlord or community. In theory they could either join their husbands or, if living in a village, obtain a grant of land to live off. In practice, however, the landlord or local authority no longer had any obligation to provide for a wife and she could only throw herself on their mercy or turn to prostitution. In addition she could not remarry until she had proof of her husband's death. Soldiers' sons could enter a military school, where they were taught a trade or joined the army when old enough; few provisions were made for soldiers' daughters.

In the first decade of the 19th century the shortest recruits were posted to the light company and tall ones to the grenadier company. From 1811 the elite companies, e.g. the light and grenadier companies, were open only to soldiers with good character and discipline who had proved themselves in battle.

Apart from their height there does not seem to have been any special requirements for enlisting in the Imperial Guard. J. Norvins, who served with the French Army at Friedland, recalls: 'Our line infantry of Ney's corps and Dupont's division fell, with the bayonet, on the Russian Imperial Guard, a formation completely recruited from northern giants … It was a victory of pygmies over giants.' When Pamfil Nazarov reached St Petersburg in 1812 he was posted to the Finlandski Guard Regiment.

Recruits drilling as shown by Wilhem Von Kobell in 1799, some of whom have not been shaved and they still wear their peasant clothes. To their front is a group of musketeers; one has the regulation calfskin knapsack while two others have linen bags instead. Note also the long queue on the soldier with his back to the reader. The officer by the side of the recruits has a cane used to beat them. This cane was abolished in 1808. (The Royal Collection © 2001 Her Majesty Queen Elizabeth II)

Soldiers became proud of their regiment, but on 31 October 1798 Paul I ordered that all the grenadier (except the Lieb Grenadiers), musketeers and Jäger regiments were known by the surname of their commander. Paul I dismissed officers frequently so that regiments regularly changed names, which was unpopular with the soldiers. In 1800 Semen Vorontsov, the Russian ambassador to England, wrote:

'I went to see the soldiers in the hospital at Portsmouth, and asked them what regiment they belonged to. A typical reply would run as follows: "I used to belong to such and such a regiment" (supplying the name). But now, little father, I don't know where I am. The Emperor has given it to some German or other.'

On 29 March 1801, Alexander I passed a law returning the regiments to their old provincial names.

TRAINING

The training for a recruit differed throughout the Napoleonic Wars, but can be divided into three distinct periods: pre-1808 training, training between 1808 and 1812 in depots, and post-1812 training.

Pre-1808 training

Training began immediately. On their journey to their regiment or recruit depot, the recruits were taught how to stand and march correctly. The conscripts' journey could last up to three months, and they marched between 20 and 30 km a day (half that distance in bad weather), and inspections took place twice a day. They were allowed to rest every third day, when they would clean and repair their clothes and might try to spend part of their allowance; public houses were to be avoided. This was also the best opportunity to desert, although with shaven forehead and, from 1808, a recruit's uniform, they were easily recognisable.

The long march was the least of the recruit's worries; from now on disease was rife; corporal punishment was meted out for any minor offence; pay, provisions and uniforms were sometimes withheld by corrupt officers. Suicide was not unknown.

A German book *A Sketch of the Russian Empire* published in 1798 recorded the recruits' sufferings:

> 'Frequently the diminution of recruits is extraordinarily great. Sometimes it happens … that in a levy of 100,000 men half of them become in three months victims of disease, or other accidents. The fatigues of their long journeys to join their corps, the immoderate use of strong liquors, the bad regime of the hospitals, are means of destruction more powerful here than in other countries … The discipline of the recruits is most severe. In peace as well as war, they are encamped from May to the end of August. There is no straw in their tents. The soldiers lie on the bare ground, cold and often humid.'

On his arrival at the regiment the recruit became a 'recruit-soldier'. To guide the new soldier through his first two years of service and make the transition to military life easier, a *diad'ka*, or uncle, was appointed by the regiment. The *diad'ka* was a soldier of at least ten years' service. It was his duty to teach the recruit-soldier how to care for his equipment, dress properly, obey the martial rules, and to understand commands and order of service. Since the recruit-soldier was often homesick the *diad'ka* was supposed to be patient, understanding and care for him; the *diad'ka* did not always perform his duties towards the conscript. After two years the recruit-soldier was considered responsible for his own actions.

Established 30 October 1808	Transferred to disbanded or January–March 1811	Division allocated to the Depot 16 March 1811
Akhtyrka		12th Division
Azov		20th Division
Belogorod	Bakhmut	9th Division
Bryansk	Starodub	7th Division
Chudnov,	Chigirin	22nd Division
Dmitrovsk	Romny	26th Division
Glukhov	Konotop	6th Division
Ivanovo		13th Division
Ivenets	Vyazma	3rd Division
Kargopol		6th Division
Kharkov	Zmiev	15th Division
Kholm		5th Division
Korosten		25th Division
Nizhnii-Novogorod	disbanded	
Novomirgorod		8th Division
Novgorod-Severski		24th Division
Olonets		21st Division
Olviopol		16th Division
Roslavl		2nd Division
Rovno	Izum	11th Division
Staraya-Russia		14th Division
Tetyushi	Taganrog	19th Division
Toropets		4th Division
Vladimir	Yelna	23rd Division
Yaroslav	Yekaterinoslav	10th Division
Zaslavl	Beloi	17th Division

For psychological reasons training camps were established throughout Russia, to help the recruit become accustomed to army life. This table shows where they were and which division they were allocated to. Note that 1st Division did not have a Recruitment Depot.

The 1798 drill book stated that, when instructing recruits, an officer or NCO was;

'Never allowed to excuse, nor forgive, their least mistake ... [they should] exercise as perfectly as an old soldier. If you neglect a recruit at the commencement ... by not passing any remarks, when he makes a mistake [he] always obstructs the others, and disturbs the entire company.'

Often as not, if a recruit did make a mistake he would be beaten. Pamfil Nazarov described his training: 'We were ordered to be taught military firearm exercises ... only from the great sorrow for my parents and the military strictness I became ill and collapsed several times a day.'

Training between 1808 and 1812 in depots

The War Ministry was aware of the physiological transition that the recruits had to go through, from tilling the fields one month to being in a regiment with its harsh discipline the next. On 30 October 1808, 27 *Zapasnyya Rekrutskiya Depo* (replacement recruit depots) were established, 'in order to avoid the deficiencies connected with the hasty distribution of recruits to regiments after their enlistment'. The depots were hundreds of miles from the recruits' homes – to prevent them deserting – and here the conscript would learn the 'basic rules of military service'. Each catered for about 2,280 recruits, divided into six companies, there being six regiments to a division. It was not until 16 March 1811 that the recruit depots were assigned to a specific division that was required to provide six officers, 24 NCOs and 240 men to train the conscripts. In November 1811, the recruit depots were formed into between four and six three-company battalions and assigned to a regiment within the division, becoming its fourth or reserve battalion of the renamed infantry regiments.

Once the recruits arrived at training camp, they were divided into small groups and began a nine-month training course in which they were introduced to army discipline. During the first two months the recruit was taught how to manoeuvre without arms; the next two with arms; in the fifth month military regulations and marching in formation; the next few months repeated what the recruit had already learnt, plus target practice; and in the final six weeks the recruit was taught how to survive on campaign, how to build a bivouac and to forage. At the end of the nine months he was ready to join his regiment.

Post-1812 training

On 27 June 1812, with the outbreak of the Patriotic War, the recruit depots were disbanded and the old system of training a recruit with a regiment was resumed.

Colonel Griois, who commanded the artillery of Grouchy's 3rd Corps in 1812, recorded in his memoirs: 'Each day we could hear section and platoon musketry which told us of the arrival of numerous recruits whom the Russian Army was hurriedly training.' After the heavy losses in the Patriotic War of 1812, Kutuzov ordered that the recruits were taught the essential manoeuvres needed, rather than elaborate parade ground

formations.

DRILL

In 1796 Paul I issued a new drill book *Military Code Concerning the Field Service for Infantry* and the following year *Tactical Rules for Military Evolutions* that were both based on the Prussian Army of Frederick the Great. Each morning and evening the roll was called and on Sundays the recruits listened while military regulations were read out.

Despite being derided by Field Marshal Suvarrov (1729–1800), Russia's leading commander, the drill book was a great leap forward in the training of the soldier. It aimed to standardise the instructions to the officers and men of the infantry and replace the individual regimental drill manuals. It not only laid down the arms drill of an infantryman, but also acted as a guide for his religious, camp and garrison life. In theory it remained in force until 1809, but like many of Paul I's reforms it was largely ignored, and after his assassination the majority of regiments resorted to their own drill book again. Regimental commanders preferred to send an officer to observe the Russian Imperial Guard drilling and manoeuvring and to record the drill movements as he perceived them. Many regiments probably preferred Field Marshal Suvarrov's *Discourse under the Trigger*, based on the regulations he wrote while colonel of the Susdal Musketeer regiment.

In 1811 the new Minister of War, Barclay de Tolly, introduced new infantry regulations which divided the recruits' schooling into three parts. The first consisting of instruction without arms, i.e. bearing, turning, marching (without bending their knees and keeping their head straight) in ordinary time (75 paces per minute) and quick time (120 paces per minute), and oblique marching. Much of this stage occurred while the recruit was marching to his new regiment or training depot.

The second part of their training was arms drill, i.e. shoulder arms, order arms etc. and the third part of the training was the manoeuvring in formation.

In 1811 *Instructions for Target Practice* prescribed that each regiment was to carry out target practice every year. Every company was to keep a list of the best marksmen. The instructor was to have 'patience' when teaching the soldiers to shoot; however, this was not always the case as Pamfil Nazarov found to his cost:

'I was conveyed to the commander of the 6th Jäger company and ordered to be instructed to shoot at a target with live cartridges. But my musket misfired, then the captain ordered a note to be made for my carelessness with the musket. After the exercise I was punished in front of the company twice with a stick.'

In 1812 Alexander I tried to issue a new drill book – based on French style drill – but this seems to have been largely ignored; it was not until after the Napoleonic Wars that Russian drill became standardised.

DISCIPLINE AND PUNISHMENT

If the *diad'ka* was considered an uncle to the recruit-soldier, then the commanding officer of the regiment was seen as a strict father. There are few documented cases of a commanding officer demonstrating care or concern for his men: one exception is M. F. Orlov, the commander of the 16th Division, who wrote to his subordinate officers 'that soldiers are people, just as we are, that they can feel and think and have virtues and that it is possible to rouse them to all that is great and glorious without sticks and beatings'. This enlightened view was exceptional. Some officers were court-martialled for cruelty, like Captain Kniazhin of the Kexholm Musketeer Regiment who was dismissed for economic abuses and inappropriate punishments in 1810; being kind to their men was seen by the authorities as a sign of weakness.

If a recruit moved, talked or held his musket wrongly twice, he would have to run the gauntlet; the soldier ran through his regiment (arranged in two ranks facing each other) as they tried to hit him with a stick. An NCO went in front and another behind, to ensure he passed through at a steady rate, while an officer made sure his comrades did not hold back. In 1806 a law established that, for petty crimes and deserting for the first time, the offender would receive 500 to 1,500 blows; on the second occasion, or for stealing an item worth over 20 roubles, he would receive 3,000 strokes; for serious crimes or deserting a third time, up to 5,000 strokes. This harsh treatment continued throughout their military life.

There was some attempt to prevent the beatings – even Alexander I condemned them in 1804 but he did little else to prevent the soldiers' sufferings. There were non-violent forms of imposing discipline: an NCO could be reduced to the ranks; a grenadier in a musketeer regiment would lose his elite status within the regiment. In theory, decorated soldiers were exempt from punishment; however, there are known cases of an officer beating decorated soldiers.

Other punishments were receiving the knout, detention in the guardhouse, riding the wooden horse or 'standing under the musket', whereby a soldier had to stand at attention for hours holding three to six muskets. The death penalty was passed for murder, rebellion and brigandage; Barclay de Tolly, commander of the 1st Western Army in 1812, sentenced several soldiers to hanging for pillaging a church.

There are examples of soldiers complaining about their treatment, but this was exceptional because the men were usually too frightened of the consequences if the officer was found not guilty.

During the Helder expedition in 1799, Lieutenant Hunt of the 7th Light Dragoons of the Anglo-Russian army particularly noted;

> 'the respect paid by the Russian soldier to their Superiors. General Hermann who was walking with the officers of his staff was observed by a party of them who was standing (in conversation) near me and at least 50 yards from their general, but the moment they saw him, their caps were off, a perfect silence and general steadiness followed.'

This respect for officers included those of the enemy, as Count Roman Soltyk of the Grande Armée in 1812 observed:

> 'I entered the house and soon found myself surrounded by about 30 Russian soldiers who were completely drunk. They did not

think of grabbing their muskets, which were propped up against the walls of the ground floor rooms. True to the respect the Russian troops have for rank, they doffed their forage caps on seeing my epaulettes and stood up as best they could, as do soldiers under arms. Their own officer could not have been better received.'

PAY AND PROVISIONS

The soldiers were paid in advance three times a year; in theory on 1 January, 1 May and 1 September. A private soldier in a field regiment during peacetime was paid nine roubles and 50 kopecks a year, a grenadier 14 roubles. During wartime a soldier would also receive a bonus for active service and acts of bravery. Despite these bonuses he was poorly paid by European standards; a Russian lieutenant received the equivalent to a private soldier in the British Army. From 1808 soldiers' pay was reduced for payments to buy medicine and support the hospitals.

Each company was divided into four sections, or *artels*. Each *artel* mustered about 35 men if the company was at full strength, was headed

Sutlers followed most armies, setting up their tent when they could, and often earned a great deal of money. Here we see members of the Russian Imperial Guard enjoying a drink. Note the lapels on the coats, the decoration on the collars and the double-headed eagle shako plate. (Courtesy of the Anne S. K. Brown University Library)

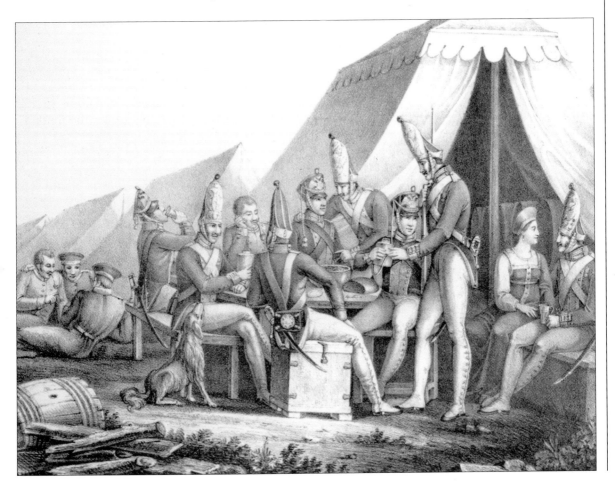

by an NCO who was assisted by five *desyalki*, and one or two of the most experienced *diad'ki*, who were 'of good morality'. In theory the company commander would appoint an *artelshchik* who would buy and distribute provisions and money to the members. However, in practice the members of each *artel* appear to have elected the *artelshchik*, usually for a term of six months.

Part of the soldiers' pay, munitions money, and any extra money they received by working or as a reward, would go towards the *artel*'s common fund; this was like a type of savings bank where the soldiers could save up for extra food or carts to carry their baggage, but they had to obtain permission from the company commander to spend it. The money was held by the company commander on trust, but there are a few cases where a dishonest commander 'borrowed' the money for his own purpose.

As well as receiving their provisions a soldier would receive 72 kopecks for meat and 24 kopecks for salt per year, which was deducted from their pay. On the march a soldier had to carry enough food for four days. In theory a daily ration was about 1 kg of grain and about 750 g of *sukhari* (a type of hard tack biscuit); bread and salt were issued on campaign. This was washed down with *kvas*, a type of beer made from bread 'steeped in hot water until it becomes acescent [sour] by fermentation', which was their favourite drink. It is known that vodka or rum was issued on occasions to keep up morale. Taking into account the religious fast days, the commissaries only ordered food for 360 days per year. However, when not on campaign or in winter quarters soldiers quartered on civilians ate what their hosts did.

The soldiers also found some very peculiar ways to supplement their diet as Lieutenant Gardner of HMS *Blonde* recorded in his journal in August 1799:

> 'We had on board a Russian captain, two subs., a surgeon, and 296 privates … They used to scrape the tallow out of the bottoms of the lanterns and make it up into balls, which they would swallow and wash down with a drink of train oil. They had bread made on purpose of the coarsest flour mixed with vinegar, and their cookery it is impossible to describe; so that the Spartan black broth must have been a luxury (however unpalatable) to their abominable messes. I have positively seen them pick the vermin off one another's jackets, which they would eat without ceremony.'

On campaign the soldier often went hungry or lived with the aid of the local inhabitants. In 1814 while in France, Paskevich wrote:

A soldier of the Imperial Guard buys some cocoa from a sutler, 1815. The word 'bistro' comes from the time of the Russians' stay in Paris. The soldiers would rush into the cafes for food and ask the proprietors to 'hurry up': to the French, the Russian word for 'quick' sounded like 'bistro'. (Courtesy of the National Army Museum)

'the grenadiers shuttling between Nangis and Troyes fed themselves as and how they could, hardly getting a crust of bread and were completely famished by all the marches and counter marches. In the morning the soldier leaves his billet hungry, not having eaten the night before; nothing is made ready for him in advance, and when he arrives at his destination he finds nothing either'.

APPEARANCE

An account describing a Russian soldier by Sir Robert Wilson leaves a vivid impression:

'The infantry is generally composed of athletic men between the ages of 18 and 40, endowed with great bodily strength, but generally of short stature, with martial countenance and complexion; inured to the extremes of weather and hardship; to the worst and scantiest food; to marches for

ABOVE **Musicians in the uniform of Paul I's reign (1796–1801) according to A. V. Viskovatov. The minimum age for company drummers was 14 years old; for flutists it was 12. During the 1807 campaign in at least one regiment, the Semenovski Guard regiment, the majority of drummers and musicians were younger than the regulation age. Other regiments probably also broke this age limit. (Author's collection)**

RIGHT **Grenadiers during the reign of Paul I according to A. V. Viskovatov. Lieutenant Colonel Dalhousie of the 2nd Royal Regiment of Foot, which served in the Helder campaign in 1799, noted; 'clothing coarse but good, buttoning before [i.e. in front] to the waist with long skirts [tails]. It is green with different coloured facings light green, light blue. I saw their artillery in scarlet. Caps are in the shape of a sugar loaf, brass front with a tuft at [the] top. Arms are an excellent firelock, a bayonet heavier than ours, a cutlass and an immense ammunition pouch'. (Author's collection)**

days and nights, of four hours repose and six hours progress; accustomed to laborious toils, and the carriage of heavy burthens; ferocious, but disciplined; obstinately brave, and susceptible of enthusiastic excitements; devoted to their sovereign, their chief, and their country.'

Paul I reintroduced the powdering of hair and A. M. Turgenev, a Russian officer, tells us what he had to go through to prepare himself for duty.

'At five o'clock in the morning I was already in the company courtyard. Two Gatchina costumiers [Gatchina was Paul I's estate, where before his accession he kept a miniature army and drilled it and dressed it according to outmoded, 18th-century styles] were already ready, experts in the art of arranging the hair according to the established style. They sat me down on a bench in the middle of a room and trimmed my hair in front close with a comb. Then one of the costumiers began to rub the front of my head with a thin sharpened piece of chalk. Five or six minutes of the costumier's vigorously rubbing my head brought me to such a state that I became afraid that I was going to be sick The wetting operation commenced. So as not to wet my undershirt, a mat sack replaced the powder gown. The costumier positioned himself exactly in front of my face, filled his mouth with some of the soldiers' home brew *kvas* beer, and began to spray my cranium as from a fire hose. As soon as he had wet me to the skull, the other costumier set to liberally sprinkling flour on my head they [then] arranged my hair with a comb and ordered me to sit still and not turn my head, thus giving time for the crown of paste on my head to dry. Behind, they tied a 15-inch rod into my hair to shape a regulation queue. They rolled my side locks into massive curls using a bent wire which encompassed my cranium and held the curled falconets on both sides, level with the middle of my ears.'

Ordinary soldiers powdered their own hair, or got one of their comrades to do it for them. A regiment had to obtain special dispensation from the Tsar not to powder their hair while on campaign.

On 9 April 1801 the lower ranks were ordered to trim their curls and have a queue 17.6 cm long, tied at the middle of the collar. On 15 July 1805 the Army of Moldavia was ordered not to powder their hair. In theory this hairstyle remained the same until 2 December 1806 when the lower ranks were ordered to cut their hair short. Before going on campaign the men were ordered to 'wash the head and the moustache and to comb the hair, until the arrival at the destination'. Despite the unpopularity of powdered hair, it was not until 6 December 1809 that it was finally abolished, although in most regiments the practice had ceased before this date.

In theory a soldier was expected to remain clean-shaven even on campaign; in practice soldiers of elite companies or regiments often grew moustaches. As early as 1802 the soldiers of the Kexholm Regiment who did not have a moustache or sideburns, fitted false ones. This practice ceased when the soldiers were ordered to grow real ones. In November 1807, the members of Semenovski regiment were ordered to

Russian Jäger grenadiers as drawn by Johann Adam Klein in Nuremberg on 4 October 1815. The soldier on the left has a white canvas knapsack, rather than the regulation leather one. The half completed figure on the right wears overalls instead of pantaloons and appears to have a camp kettle strapped to his knapsack. (Courtesy of Museen der Stadt Nuremberg)

Group of Jäger grenadiers of 41st regiment, seen by Johann Adam Klein on 19 March 1815. The figure in the centre is wearing grey trousers with a red stripe down the outside, which were worn by officers on campaign. The officer also appears to have an NCO's pompon on his shako. (Courtesy of Museen der Stadt Nuremberg)

wear their moustaches 'uninterrupted', i.e. joined to their sideburns, but with visible cheeks. The fashion seems to have spread quickly to the grenadiers of all regiments to mark their elite status; in August 1809 it was forbidden for them to shave off their moustache and sideboards. Later, the regiment hairstyle became the choice of its commanding officer. The regiment's barber would shave a soldier every two or three days, or before a solemn occasion. Ensign Ivan Kazakov, an officer in the Russian Army of Occupation in 1814, recorded that while in bivouac in Paris 'the doctor's assistants shaved the soldiers, others shaved themselves before immense mirrors and dyed their moustaches'.

Jägers and jäger grenadiers of the 38th Jäger regiment at Nuremberg on 28 May 1815. The numbers on their shoulder straps should be 'three' because they formed part of the 3rd Brigade. (Courtesy of Museen der Stadt Nuremberg)

Uniforms and equipment

A regiment was provided with or given enough money to buy cloth and leather to produce its own uniforms by the state. Soldiers usually made their own as tailors and artisans could be found in the ranks. The men had to pay for any lost items. This system was open to abuse: in 1810 an officer of the Kexholm Musketeer regiment issued second-hand uniforms to his men, and soldiers had to buy new uniforms from their regimental savings. There are also instances of officers either using money from regimental funds or paying for uniforms out of their own pocket when governmental issue was not forthcoming. According to the 1797 drill book, uniforms were issued on 1 May each year; however, there is some evidence to suggest that this was later changed to 'the end of the year' or 24 December.

Soldiers of a grenadier regiment drawn by Johann Adam Klein on 30 May 1815. (Courtesy of Museen der Stadt Nuremberg)

In *Secret memoir* C. Masson compared the appearance of the infantry during Catherine the Great's reign (1762–96) and that of Paul I's (1796–1801):

'The Russian army offered a pattern to be followed, in the beauty, simplicity and convenience of its dress, equally adapted to the climate and to the genius of the country … The soldier was dressed in the twinkling of an eye for he had but two garments and their size was such as allowed him to defend himself from the cold by additions underneath, without infringing upon the uniformity of his external appearance. This neat and warlike equipage is now changed for the ancient dress of Germany, which the Russian soldier abominates; his fair locks, which he loved to wash every morning, he must now bedaub with grease and flour, and he must spend an hour buttoning his black gaiters which he curses for pinching his legs.'

Reginald Heber, the Bishop of Calcutta who journeyed through Russia in 1805, observed that the soldiers wore a belt 'around the waist, which is tied so ridiculously tight as very much to impede the free use of the limbs; on the whole their dress is, like that of most other soldiers, more fit for a parade than actual service.'

Coats were issued every two years and greatcoats every four years. The greatcoats were single breasted made from undyed or white cloth during Paul I's reign and during Alexander I's (1801–1825) beige, dark or light grey cloth was also introduced. However, whatever the shade each regiment was to have the same colour, with the collar and shoulder straps the same as the coat. According to A. V. Viskovatov on 14 July 1808 it was ordered that in:

'the warm or good weather, the soldier was to have his greatcoat rolled over his left shoulder, with the ends low on his right side being tied with a whitened deerskin strap. In cold weather it was ordered to wear the greatcoat with all its buttons fastened and to take off the coat and place it behind the back above the waist, between the skirt and greatcoat. But in frosts, the coat was to be worn in addition to the greatcoat.'

On 20 April 1809 additional regulations laid down that the greatcoat should be rolled 16 cm wide and tied 8 cm from the ends with a strap.

Soldiers were issued with a new pair of pantaloons and a pair of linen trousers every year; their trousers appear to have lasted on average six months. During the summer this was inconvenient, but in winter, especially that of 1812, the lack of trousers could prove disastrous, as Sir Robert Wilson notes:

'out of 10,000 recruits afterwards marched on Wilna as a reinforcement, only 1500 reached that city; the greater part of these were conveyed to hospitals as sick or mutilated. One of the chief causes of their losses was that the trousers becoming worn by the continued marches in the inner part of the thighs exposed the flesh, so that the frost struck into it when chafed and irritated it with virulent activity.'

On campaign, despite repeated protests from the high command, some soldiers wore baggy linen overalls to protect their trousers. Although recorded by artists like Johann Adam Klein, it is not clear how common this practice was.

The soldiers were issued with two pairs of black leather boots with two extra pairs of soles, three pairs of linen or woollen puttees or

Sketch by C. J. Erhard dated 1815. Captain Mercer in 1815 recorded that the Russians were dressed in a 'dirty forage cap, as dirty a grey greatcoat, generally gathered back by the waist, so as to be out of the way, [and] dirty linen trousers'. This soldier wears campaign overalls underneath his greatcoat. (Courtesy of Anne S K Brown University Library)

Pavlov grenadier and officer, according to A. V. Viskovatov. When shakos were introduced in 1805 the private soldiers of the Pavlov Grenadiers were allowed to keep their mitre type grenadier caps as a mark of their bravery. In May 1825, for the sake of uniformity, the officers of the Pavlov Grenadier Regiment were ordered to wear the mitre; up to this point bicorns and then shakos had been worn. (Author's collection)

Each regiment had a large number of non-combatant soldiers, including barbers, blacksmiths and hospital attendants. This print shows two of these soldiers in their 1812 grey uniform. (Author's collection)

stockings, and three linen shirts with a small detachable collar and cuffs fastened by buttons or tape.

In July 1813 Colonel (Sir Hudson) Lowe, a British liaison officer with the Prussian General Blucher's staff (who later became Napoleon's gaoler at St Helena), described the accoutrements of the infantry as:

'in general of bad leather without any proper inside case to hold the cartridges and keep them dry, and not holding conveniently more than 40 rounds, but the men were accustomed to keep the cartridges rolled up in packages of ten each and to put up what the pouch did not hold in their packs. The packs are of leather, small and not ill made, if they can be rendered proof against the rain'.

The cartridge box was also designed to carry spare parts for the musket and flints: it was waterproofed with wax to prevent the cartridges becoming damp.

In 1802 cylindrical black leather knapsacks replaced the calfskin one introduced by Paul I in 1797. On 14 July 1808 a rectangular one was introduced which continued in service until the end of the Napoleonic Wars. However, the knapsacks were not waterproofed, and often captured French knapsacks of calfskin were worn. Linen bags were also used as a substitute for the leather knapsacks. On the back of the knapsack was a tin canteen for carrying liquor.

According to A. V. Viskovatov, a knapsack was meant to carry;

'two shirts, a pair of trousers, a pair of foot wraps, a forage cap, material for a pair of boots, a frizzen cover, 12 flints, three brushes, two scrapers, a small board for cleaning buttons, a small quantity of chalk and polish, a small valise with threads, soap, glue, needle case with needles, moustache dye, dye comb, sand and a brick, and rusks for three days, so that the valise with the canteen and summer trousers weighed 25 pounds, but with the winter trousers (instead of summer) 26.25 pounds.'

During the reign of Paul I musketeers and jägers wore the bicorn hat, while the grenadiers and fusiliers wore the mitre cap, with a metal front in the colour of the regiment's buttons.

In September 1802 shakos were introduced into the Jäger regiments. They were also issued to the musketeers in August 1803, replacing their bicorn hats. In 1805 a new style of shako was introduced to all three branches of infantry, e.g. jägers, musketeers and grenadiers. However, some musketeers still wore their bicorns at the Battle of Austerlitz and many grenadiers their mitre caps. The Pavlov regiment were still wearing mitres in 1807; during that year the regiment showed such bravery at the Battle of Friedland, that Alexander I allowed them to continue wearing them.

In June 1809 shako cords were issued, but they were usually removed on campaign. In 1812 a new type of shako was introduced, being issued straight away to some, as the 5th Tirailleurs observed at the Battle of Smolensk: 'Russian grenadiers, [were] recognisable by the three copper flames on their very low and concave shakos.' The Elberfeld manuscript, produced during 1813 and 1814, shows a Russian grenadier wearing an 1807 style shako (a restyling of the 1805 type, to include black leather top bands, and V-shaped reinforcements on the sides). Shakos were issued every two years; those who were issued one in 1811 would have to wait until 1813 for their new shako. In theory new recruits would be issued with the new form of shako, so there were two types of shakos present in each regiment between 1812 and 1814.

Protective shako covers were officially introduced in May 1817; black or butternut coloured ones of linen soaked in wax, are known to have been worn in 1814, and probably much earlier. After chinstraps were introduced for the shako it was often used as a bucket to gather provisions, and soon became deformed.

In *History of the Campaign in France*, General Mikhailovsky-Danielevsky records:

'There was such a scarcity of uniforms and shoes, that out of Prince Eugene of Wurttemburg's entire corps, it was hardly possible to pick out a thousand men decently enough clothed and shod In their exterior, Raiefski's troops had more the look of Frenchmen than Russians, as the men, on joining from the reserves in grey jackets, had lost no time in exchanging them for French uniforms, which they stripped from the backs of the killed and prisoners.'

Captain Alexander Cavalié Mercer, a British officer in the Royal Horse Artillery, was in Paris in 1815 with the occupation force that included a Russian contingent:

'I see hundreds of their soldiers (infantry) without bestowing on them the slightest attention. These, smart as they are on the parade, are the dirtiest slovens in the world off it; the usual costume in which one sees them running about la Chapelle is a dirty forage cap, as dirty a grey greatcoat, generally gathered back by the waist-strap, so as to be out of the way, dirty linen trousers, shoved up at the bottom by the projection of the unlaced half boot.'

Arms

There were 28 different types of musket in use among the infantry of varying quality. In 1805 Reginald Heber paid a visit to the St Petersburg arsenal:

'Here as well as at Petrozovodsky, in the government of Olonetz and at Susterbeck in Carelia, is the manufacture of arms. All the

RIGHT **Soldiers wearing forage caps marching to Borna, Saxony, during May 1801. (© Musée de L'Armée, Paris, 2001)**

BELOW **The regimental march of the Pskov Musketeer regiment, which was renamed the General Field Marshal Prince Kutuzov of Smolensk's Pskov Infantry regiment as a tribute to Kutuzov, who had been the honorary colonel from 1799 until his death in 1813. As well as the official marches the soldiers also sang about the campaigns they had fought in, their heroes and their mistreatment.**

Russian muskets, their screws, locks, stocks, worm-pickers and all others [of] the most minute parts are made in conformity to an exact gauge; by this excellent system nothing is wasted, as from two or three useless muskets they may always make one good one, and the sound parts of their unserviceable arms may be always made use of for the repair of others.'

At the Tula Arsenal Heber got a very different view of Russian muskets:

'The guns made here look very neat, but the springs, locks etc. are all bad, and the guns very apt to burst when they are discharged. A tolerable musket may be bought for two or three guineas English. In these latter works they usually make 1,200 muskets a week; and

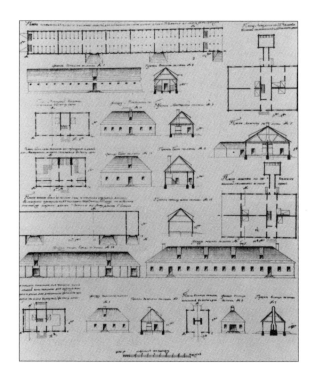

RIGHT **Plan of a barrack block for infantry. Lieutenant Colonel John Johnson, who toured Russia in 1817, wrote the barracks 'are built of timber-hewn square, laid flat on one another and mortised at the corners. The windows and doors are cut out of the side that faces inwards; the former are frequently covered with paper instead of glass. The roofs consist usually of long slips of bark spread open and fastened down by long battens laid across them to prevent warping'.**

in case of need can supply a regiment which may demand about 1,600. The present Emperor [Alexander I] has, since the affair of Austerlitz, sent down a new model. The musket, without the bayonet weighting only 10.5 pounds, English. The wood used in making them is supplied by considerable woods in a low swampy tract of country, which abounds in the province to the south.'

This new musket was the 1808 pattern with a 17.78 mm calibre and was 145.8 cm long (183 cm with the bayonet) and weighed 4.47 kg and fired a 23.8 g ball, as compared to the 1798 pattern musket which weighed about 7.5 kg. Jäger regiments carried the 1805 rifle with the sword bayonet, it had a polygonal barrel with eight grooves and it had a 16.51 mm calibre and weighed 4.09 kg. Muskets were also imported, including Brown Besses and Baker Rifles from Britain, which were issued to the best troops.

DAILY LIFE

When not on active service the regiment would be dispersed into winter quarters. Although some barracks existed, the men were usually quartered on peasant families in towns or villages. The peasants were obliged to feed the soldiers and were, in theory, reimbursed at a later date.

While the soldiers were in these billets there was sometimes tension between soldiers and civilians, which could lead to unrest. However, a soldier might also meet a partner: as long as she was of 'good conduct and honest' he was free to marry her – subject to his commanding officer's permission.

When quartered for a long time the soldiers would construct a Turkish bath; these vapour baths were a common pastime for serf and nobility alike. Other pastimes included dancing, chess and draughts, wrestling and a type of 'football' that records described as follows: 'a large ball stuffed with feathers is kicked about, and he who succeeds in catching it, or picking it up with his hands, in spite of the kicks and cuffs of his playmates carries off the prize'.

Singing was a favourite pastime, either on the march or when they had been dismissed for the day, and it also had the benefit of keeping up morale. The night before the Battle of Borodino an officer attached to Prince Karl von Mecklenburg's staff was with the Fanagoria grenadiers and noted in his diary:

'The soldiers were in fairly good order, and ... they now sat, wrapped in their long grey [great]coats, round the fires, and often joined in chorus to sing the monotonous, melancholy, dirge-like, yet not unpleasing national songs which the Russian people are so fond of. This singing before the battle had a strange effect on me, and I listened to it for several hours until eventually I fell asleep.'

On very rare occasions a soldier might be given leave. Trooper Ivan Minaev (who has left the one of only two accounts of a private Russian soldier during the Napoleonic Wars) was lucky enough to be granted

A NCO of a Jäger regiment guarding a somewhat idealised campsite, by A. V. Viskovatov. Sir Robert Wilson, an English general attached to the Russian staff, describes that a soldier on campaign had 'no other bed than the snow, no shelter but the heavens, and no other coverings but their rags'. (Author's collection)

leave and, unusually, was able to return to his village where he was greeted by his family who admired him in his uniform.

In the spring the regiment would muster for manoeuvres and regimental drill; during the summer the divisions and corps would gather for six weeks for additional exercises and manoeuvres. In 1813 it was recommended that soldiers were drilled for two to three hours in the morning and again in the afternoon, each day except for Saturdays and Sundays.

There were regulations for religious services; matins and vespers had to be sung each day and on Wednesdays, Sundays and holidays, soldiers had to attend Mass. Large tents were supplied where the services were held. Martha Wilmot observed: 'At the rising and setting of the sun and on other occasions they begin to cross themselves, but so *obstreperously* that the operation does not finish under quarter of an hour.' Each regiment also had a priest, two altar boys and probably its own icon.

The Russians were also superstitious. One British officer in the Helder believed that the Russians were defeated at the Battle of Bergen because they 'considered this an unlucky day'.

In peacetime the colonel of the regiment could also use up to a third of his men to work on his estate, or even 'hire them out to private individuals and keep their earnings by right'. Writing in 1819, Major Don Juan van Halen, a Spaniard in Russian service, records a custom that had become standard practice long before the Napoleonic Wars:

A print depicting three members of the Imperial Guard. Although this image is dated 1812, the Pavlov Grenadiers were not incorporated into the Guard until 1813. Moreover the regiment did not receive its Guard's uniform until 1814. (Courtesy of the Borodino Museum)

Imperial Guard NCO, 1815: for all private soldiers this rank is the most they could hope to achieve.

'The soldiers … become masons, carpenters, smiths etc. or engaged in whatever occupation they may be hired for: … they are furnished by the colonel with suitable dress so that their uniforms may not suffer during the time they are thus employed, they cannot be recognised as soldiers except by their moustaches. Besides, there are always a certain number of men employed in the workshops belonging to the regiment in every description of trade: consequently everything that can possibly be wanted in the corps is made by the soldiers.'

The practice of outside work (*volnyye raboty*) was prohibited by Alexander I, but as the custom continued the Tsar altered his policy so that soldiers should not carry out dangerous work. There is evidence to suggest that the private soldier benefited from this work; it not only cut down on boredom, but any money was divided between the men involved and the soldiers' *artel* – the sum having been negotiated between the officer and the *artelshchik* beforehand.

Apart from occasional bonuses for bravery, there were few rewards for a private soldier for good conduct. According to 1796 regulations, nobles had to serve three years as an NCO as part of

ABOVE **A dead Russian soldier who had been sniping at a battery of Wurttemburg artillery, during the Grande Armée's invasion of Russia. Faber du Faur, an artist and officer in the battery, recorded: 'Next day, 9 August [1812], visiting the spot out of pure curiosity, we found our enemy's body lying face downward among the broken and splintered trees. He had been killed by one of our roundshots.' (Courtesy of Russian State Museum)**

ABOVE **A grenadier of a musketeer regiment in campaign dress. He wears the non-regulation baggy overalls which were common throughout the army. (Author's collection)**

their officer training, whereas peasants had to serve at least 12 years to reach this rank. In 1798, Tsar Paul I forbade any NCOs with peasant origins becoming officers since this would ennoble them. In 1806, due to high casualties, this changed: nobles served three months as privates, and three months as an NCO before promotion to officer status, although the noble was not usually present with the army during this period. The new regulations meant that the peasant-soldier was even more excluded from the rank of NCO. In 1811 reforms in the army allowed soldiers who had distinguished themselves in battle and were of good conduct to transfer to the grenadier regiments, thus making them elite units.

For those who did not get promotion for faithful service there were several awards. The Order of St Anne was awarded for 20 years good service and, from 1807, the Order of St George was awarded for bravery. Recipients were also awarded a pension. Other medals were awarded for battles and campaigns: C. Masson wrote: 'I have seen whole regiments, where none but the recruits just arrived were without them.' Only the Emperor could deny an award for misconduct, such as insubordination or drunkenness. In March 1825 good service awards allowed soldiers to wear one yellow tape on the left arm for ten years service, two for 15 years and three for 20 years.

RIGHT **Pursuit of the Grande Armée in 1812. In reality the Russians suffered great hardship from the weather: they lost over 75 percent of their total force during the winter of 1812. (Courtesy of the Russian State Museum)**

After Ulm's surrender Captain James Ramsey, a British liaison officer with the Russian Army at Brunn, wrote on 9 November 1805:

> 'The Russian troops are marching through this town, partly in wagons part on foot. They go at the rate of 40 English miles a day. I have just seen 5,000 men pass through of the finest infantry I have ever seen. They are also in the highest spirits and by no means discouraged by the event which has taken place.'

Tensions between the Austrians and Russians during the Austerlitz campaign led the Austrians to claim that the Russians were leaving a path of plundered villages in their trail, but this was not always the case. Usually they did plunder in enemy territory, but in friendly territory they mostly behaved well. According to Reginald Heber, during the Austerlitz campaign the 'Russians were popular among the common people, which at once proved the falsehood of the scandals circulated against them at Vienna'.

The Russian disliked having allies, although they were necessary to defeat the Grande Armée. In 1805 they were contemptuous of their Austrian allies, and in the later stages of the Napoleonic Wars, the Russians accused the Prussians of backwardness in the campaigns of 1813 and 1814, especially after the Battle of Laon, where they believed Blucher failed to press home his attack. According to Captain Friedrich von Schubert, a Russian officer from a German émigré family who was attached to the Russian General Staff:

> 'Our soldiers had a kind of good-natured contempt for the Prussians: they were *nemzy* [dumb]; but among the generals and officers matters were more serious. The King of Prussia liked us, but his generals did not ... a war between the Russians, with the French as allies, and the Prussians would have been welcomed with delight throughout the Russian army; we liked the French much better than the Prussians.'

In July 1813 the new recruits of the Finlandski Guard Regiment, including Pamfil Nazarov, had finished their training and were ordered to join the army. According to Pamfil Nazarov they pursued the enemy:

> 'Across Silesia, Bohemia and Saxony to the town of Dresden near to which the enemy gave battle, which continued for two days, the cannonade and musketry battle took place in foul weather. We commenced firing bombs to set the town alight until His Imperial Majesty ordered the Guards Corps to retreat along two roads to the town of Teplitz, the first division [took] the main road and ours, the second division, the country road. For us this road being awkward, by reason of the woods and marshes, and the enemy pressing us in pursuit, our artillery and horse dislodged us from the road and we were forced to go into the marshes ... We began the retreat from the town at 9 o'clock in the evening and

Private, Moscow Grenadiers, Smolensk Inspection, 1805

A

B

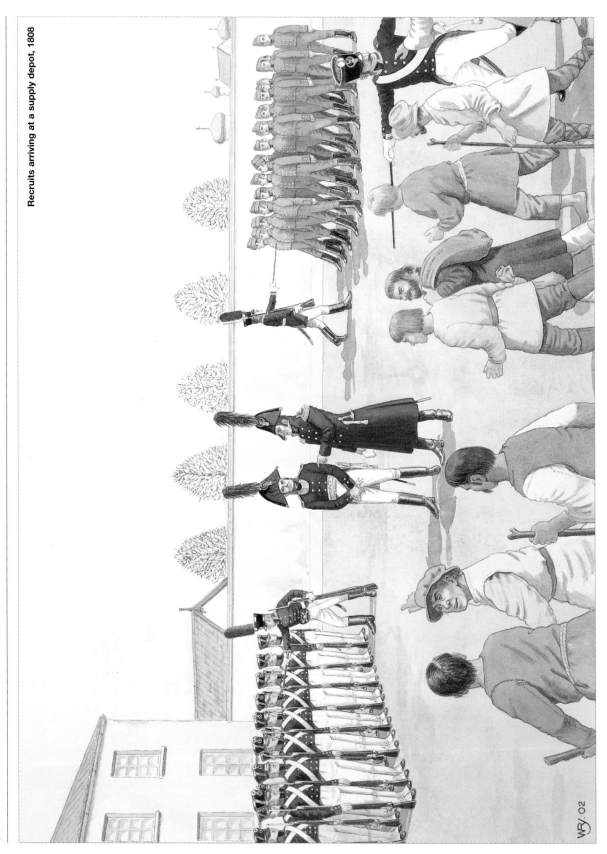

Recruits arriving at a supply depot, 1808

WRY. 02

Discipline and punishment, 1807

C

D

A company of the **Narva Regiment, 12th Division**, advances into battle, 1812

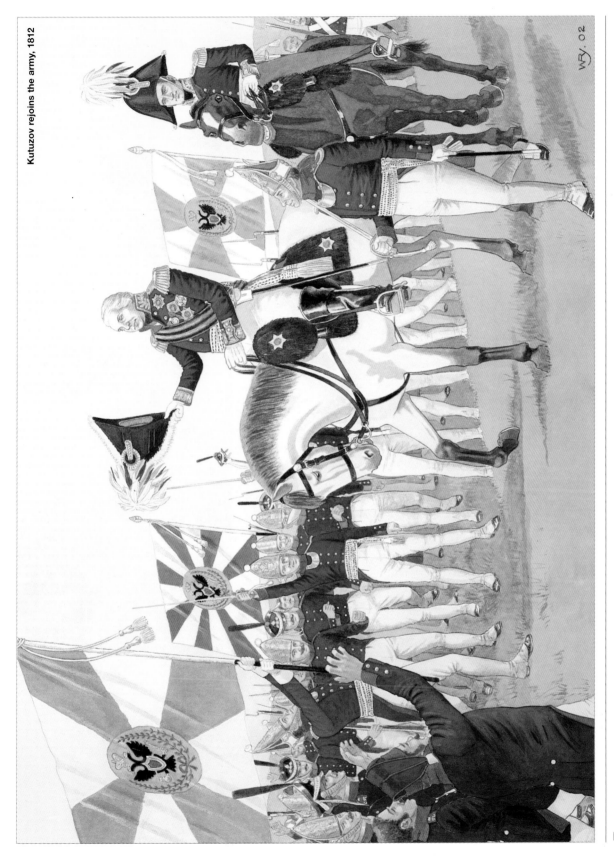

Kutuzov rejoins the army, 1812

WFY. 02

E

The Battle of Borodino, 7 September 1812

F

The camp at Taruntino, 1812

Private, Moscow Grenadiers, 1812

H

continued until 8 o'clock in the morning, approaching a hamlet, which being not more than ten houses, by them we made ourselves comfortable in the fields to cook.'

Von Plotho, a Prussian officer, records that when the Russian soldier 'gets to his camp or bivouac, he digs a hole in the ground, puts a base mat in it, pours his flour on top, mixes it with water, heats up a second pit, and so bakes his bread … If the Russian has a little salt, or an onion and a cucumber, and some kvas … this provides him with a splendid meal'. Often soldiers did not have time to cook their meagre rations and could be ordered to retreat in an instant.

The retreat of the Grande Armée. The severity of the conditions of the winter of 1812 are clear.

Marching

On 22 February 1803 ordinary time march rate of a Russian infantryman was set at 75 paces per minute, and quick time at 120. These rates, however, were slower than their French counterparts (whose ordinary time was 76 paces per minute), which resulted in the French out-marching the Russians. To prevent the French catching the Russians on the march, rearguard actions were necessary; most notably at Schongrabern on 16 November 1805, when Bagration gave Kutuzov's main body a chance to escape. By 1807 two more steps had been introduced: triple time, of 200 to 250 paces per minute, and a fourth step used on campaign when soldiers could relax and march at their ease.

Sickness

A soldier was more likely to succumb to disease rather than become a casualty in battle. During 1799 and 1800 the Edinburgh Military Hospital treated 243 Russian patients from the Helder campaign where disease spread rapidly due to wet weather. None of the soldiers were wounded in battle: 112 had a fever (probably typhus) from which 24 died; 45 had scurvy; 13 had diarrhoea; two had sexually transmitted diseases; others had various complaints like pneumonia and leg injuries.

A Soviet demographer, B. C. Urlanis, believed that the Russian Army suffered 110,000 deaths from the effects of battle during the campaign of 1812, whereas 140,000 were wounded or died of disease, almost a quarter of a million men. Other estimates vary between 660,000 to two million men who were killed, died of wounds or sickness. It was reported to Alexander I that, due to disease and casualties, the army renewed its personnel every five or six years.

Desertion

Desertion was a problem on campaign; the fear of punishment for the loss of equipment or harsh treatment made many desert. C. Masson wrote:

'Before the reign of Paul I desertion was almost unknown; now they desert in parties and repair to Prussia, where whole regiments are formed. I asked some of them why they deserted.

"Why, Sir?" said they "we are forced to be at our exercise from morning till night without having anything to eat; our dress has been taken from us and we are beaten black and blue."'

The Persian Army recruited Russian deserters who were considered the best soldiers in the army. Serfs were offered rewards to capture deserters roaming the countryside; once returned to his regiment a deserter could expect to be severely punished.

Motivation and morale

The constant state of war between France, Turkey, Persia and Sweden took its toll on the effectiveness of the regiments. Over the years the quality of recruits gradually declined. In his memoirs Captain Friederich von Schubert compared the army of 1807 to that of 1812:

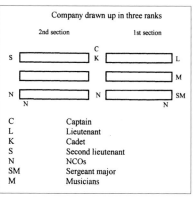

Diagram of how an infantry company was drawn up in three ranks and in two sections.

'every man knew one thing only … his duty was to hold any position allotted to him to the death. The feeling of invincibility pervaded in the Army like a creed, and every misfortune, every lost battle was ascribed to treachery … A division or regiment which has had the same commander for a long time, which has been through difficult times with him and won victories, is proud of him and will, out of attachment to him gladly endure privations, which would not be tolerated out of mere obedience; with him the division or regiment will easily overcome obstacles which they would not even have attempted to overcome under anyone else's command. The state of the Russian Army in 1806 lasted more or less until the war of 1812–1814, at which point it was substantially altered. The constant wars had taken away many of the old soldiers, and the young ones did not have the same traditions; nor could they feel the same attachment to their corps as the old ones did'.

Barclay de Tolly, also had noticed the decline in the Russian Army, writing in 1810:

'In place of strong and brave troops, our regiments consist in large measure of green soldiers, unaccustomed to the rigours of war. The present prolonged war has smothered their traditional heroic virtues. Their patriotism, as well as their physical strength, have begun to weaken with the beginning of this intense and useless war.'

While on St Helena Napoleon agreed with these statements: he was reported as saying 'the Russian Army which fought at Austerlitz would not have lost the Battle of Borodino'.

The Smolensk Infantry regiment is just one example of the decline in the Russian Army mentioned by von Schubert and Barclay de Tolly. On 10 October 1812 it mustered just 852 rank and file, of whom 247 came from the Opolchenie (the newly raised militia), 413 were recruits, leaving 192 veterans. The regiment was further reduced during the pursuit of the Grande Armée and the subsequent campaigns. Early in 1813 some regiments mustered just 150 men.

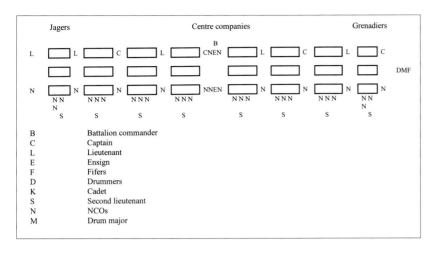

Jagers	Centre companies	Grenadiers

B   Battalion commander
C   Captain
L   Lieutenant
E   Ensign
F   Fifers
D   Drummers
K   Cadet
S   Second lieutenant
N   NCOs
M   Drum major

A battalion drawn up in line, three ranks deep with the elite companies on each flank. As the Napoleonic Wars progressed the linear formations in battle declined in favour of the column.

TACTICS

Organisation

The structure of a Russian infantry regiment was composed of elite troops: grenadiers recruited from the tallest men, and light infantry (used for skirmishing) were the smallest in the regiment. The 'centre' companies were formed from the rest of the recruits.

In November 1796 infantry regiments were divided into two battalions, each with a grenadier company and five musketeer companies. In grenadier regiments the musketeers companies were replaced by fusiliers. In 1798 the jäger battalions were formed into regiments of two battalions each of five jäger companies. On 30 April 1802 all infantry regiments were 'ordered to consist of three, four-company battalions; the Life Grenadiers of three grenadier battalions, other grenadiers regiments of one grenadier and two fusilier battalions; Musketeer [regiments] of one grenadier and two musketeer battalions; Jägers of three jäger battalions'. Each company was divided into two sections or platoons.

When Barclay de Tolly became Minister of War, he reorganised the army along French lines. In October 1810 he ordered that the infantry regiments, like grenadier regiments, were to have three battalions each of one grenadier and three Fusilier companies. The musketeer regiments, (renamed infantry) were to have three battalions of one grenadier and three musketeer companies. The Jäger battalions were to have one jäger-grenadier and three jäger companies. Another French innovation introduced at this time was the corps system, which grouped two divisions together. The divisions were usually formed of three brigades each of two regiments.

Before 1810 all battalions of a regiment had taken the field, but now only the first and third were to serve in a campaign. The centre companies of the second battalion were used to bring the other two battalions up to strength. To mark their new role the second battalion was renamed a *Zapasnyi* (or replacement battalion). The grenadier companies from these battalions were united with the other grenadier companies of the second battalions of their division to form a Combined Grenadier battalion each of three companies. These battalions formed a Combined Grenadier Brigade used as the reserve.

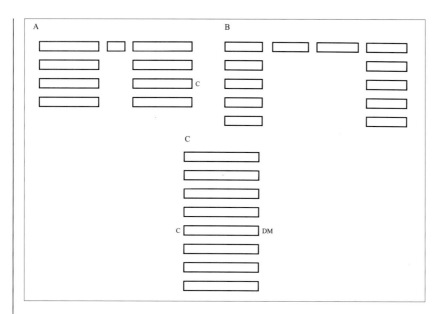

A. Column of companies, which was common throughout the Napoleonic Wars. B. A mixed column where one battalion drew up in line and two others in column, as used by the Russians at Eylau and Borodino. C. Another common formation in the Napoleonic Wars was the column of sections, which had a shorter frontage and more depth than the column of companies. Column formations were easier to control than the line: howerver they lacked firepower, with only the first company or section being able to fire.

The grenadier company's first platoon consisted of grenadiers and the second platoon, jägers or light infantry. From 1811 the grenadiers and riflemen were men chosen 'despite their height, for excellent behaviour, constancy and endurance in work, courage and bravery'. The smaller men went to the jägers, the taller ones to the grenadiers, and the weaker ones, whatever their size, formed the centre companies.

Formations

Paul I's drill book of 1796 describes the drawing up of a regiment as follows:

> 'When a battalion or an entire regiment go to exercise they shall always divide each company in two platoons [in four]... for special reviews or for church parade. The battalion is always composed of ten platoons. In all events the grenadiers forming a battalion by themselves and the regiment remains invariably composed of two battalions.
> 'When a battalion or a regiment is in battle with open ranks, at that time the distance between the ranks is to be of four small paces.'

The 1811 new infantry regulations introduced by the War Ministry described the drawing up of a regiment as follows:

> 'Infantry regiments consist of three battalions, which are numbered 1st, 2nd and 3rd, when the regiment is drawn up in battle order, the first battalion is on the right flank, near it is placed the 2nd and then the 3rd battalion. Each battalion consists of four companies ... Each company is divided into two platoons (*Vzvod*). In the grenadier company the first platoon consists of grenadiers and the second of riflemen. The other companies are also divided into two platoons, of which one is called the first and the other the second.
> 'When the battalion is drawn up in battle formation, the grenadier platoon forms up on the right flank of the battalion, by

it … the three musketeer companies and finally the platoon of riflemen which stands on the left flank of the battalion. The Platoon is divided into half platoons and by sections. In the section is found not less than four and not more than six files.'

It was prescribed that the most experienced and brave men were to be in the front rank, the rear rank was to be formed from the old and reliable soldiers and the middle or second rank to be formed of new soldiers of doubtful quality. Those on the flanks were to be the best within the company.

Paul I's drill book recommended linear formations of three ranks. Although linear formations were good for defensive actions, they quickly became disordered once the line advanced. If ordered to advance the regiment would quickly form a column.

As well as the official manuals for drawing up a regiment in battle formation there were also unofficial guides. Baron Antoine-Henri de Jomini (a general in the Grande Armée who subsequently became a general in Russian service) published *Traite des grandes operations militaires* in 1804, while A. I. Khatov's *General Survey of Tactics and Basic Principles of Military Tactics*, published between 1807 and 1810, was largely based on Guibert's 1773 *Essai generale de tactique*. Both Jomini and Khatov recommended the use of column formations in 'battalions by divisions of two companies' rather than linear tactics. In a later edition of his work Jomini recorded the Russians 'formed columns of four divisions in three ranks … the skirmishers are taken from the third rank of each division, which makes a column of eight men in depth instead of 12 and gives move mobility'.

Kutuzov favoured columns. On 18 October 1805 he wrote that 'it will often be necessary to form battalion columns, whether to pass through a line, or to deliver an attack more effectively in difficult terrain'. Furthermore:

'We shall often have to exploit the peculiar prowess of the Russians in bayonet attacks. The following points are therefore to be noted and obeyed with the greatest exactitude:
'1. The cry of "*oorah*" is one that brings us victory. Nobody is to dare utter it until the command is given by the brigade commander, at the very lowest point.'
'2. During the attack with the bayonet the front of the formation is to be held as straight as possible, so that nobody will run ahead.'
'3. Upon the command "Halt! Dress!" the battalions will come to an instant stop'.

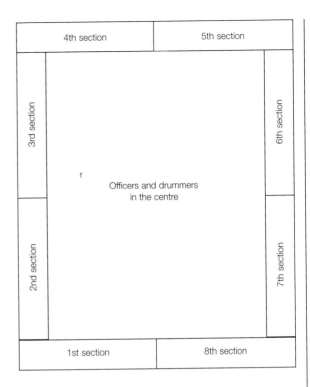

4th section		5th section	
3rd section	Officers and drummers in the centre		6th section
2nd section			7th section
1st section		8th section	

Like infantry of other nationalities the infantry square was used to receive cavalry. It was used to great effect in the wars against Turkey, although considered too dangerous to use in Europe where artillery was more numerous.

Although there were regiments and companies of jägers, grenadiers and musketeers, even the militia (Opolochenie) could also be called upon to skirmish with mixed results.

In 1807 the practice was to form up in columns of companies (also known as column of divisions) and in exceptional circumstances columns of sections. A column of companies would be 12 men deep, each company being three men deep with a frontage of about 60 men, if at full strength, with gaps between each company. Each man stood shoulder to shoulder with his comrades.

Another formation was the *ordre mixte* whereby one regiment or battalion would be drawn up in line with two others drawn up in column behind the flanks of the line. Benningsen used this type of formation at the Battle of Friedland in 1807 and by some units at Borodino in 1812. According to General Jomini this formation 'might, according to circumstances, be as good for the offensive as for the defensive'.

When attacking in echelon the aim 'of the first attack should be to endeavour to gain the enemy's flank'. If retreating the odd number battalions of the Division or brigade (numbered from the right) would retreat, while the 'even numbers cover those retreating and turning the flanks of its platoons in order to cross fire to defend the intervals abandoned by the retreating battalions'. Once the odd numbered battalions had retreated 150 to 200 paces, then it was the even numbered battalions' turn to retreat.

In his memoirs Thadeusz Kosciuszko, who led a Polish uprising against the Russians during the early 1790s, recorded that the Russians.'

'most frequent manoeuvres are to form a straight line, to march by battalions and divisions, and to change front and form square, which they unfailingly do when they are under pressure. Their main principle of war is to get their attack first, which they often perform in several columns. They advance confidently enough, but when they are attacked in their turn their only recourse is to form square, in which formation they hold out until the bitter end.'

The tactic of forming square had been used to good effect in Russia's wars with the Persians and Turks, who had a large percentage of cavalry in their armies. When it came to fighting European adversaries this tactic was considered far too dangerous. The French had a greater percentage of artillery and infantry in their armies, so the Russian squares were an easy target, as seen at the Battle of Bergen on 19 September 1799, when the French counter-attacked and overran the Russian squares. In 1807 the Russian War Ministry considered that 'in battles with European regular forces the square formation is exceedingly dangerous … [because it] presents a great target for the enemy's artillery'. The square was still used to receive cavalry and in Russia's wars with Turkey; according to Captain von Schubert, at the Battle of Schumen in 1810 the Russian squares were 'like so many rocks in an ocean of cavalry' and that in their frustration some Turkish cavalry actually dismounted to fight the Russians hand to hand.

Skirmishing

Whatever the formation adopted on the battlefield it was covered by a screen of light infantry. Little was officially written on skirmishing tactics during the Napoleonic Wars. A document from the Russian War Ministry entitled *Instructions to the infantry officers on the day of battle* dated 29 July 1812 states:

'An officer commanding the skirmishes sent in front of the troops may not move his chain forward without permission from his regimental or battalion commander; his duty is to hide his men if possible, but he himself must move incessantly along the chain as much for the supervision of the enemy movements and enemy mounted skirmishers charging at him. Having let them come within 150 paces the officer must fire and, if he sees that he has not stopped them by fire, at a signal he will get his men together in groups of ten back to back. In this position he will continue to fire and stab the approaching horsemen with bayonets in full confidence that his battalion or regiment will rush forward to help them.'

It was not until 1818 that skirmishing was officially referred to in training manuals. The *Regimental training rules* (1818) suggested that the chain of skirmishes should be 300 paces from the battalion. Before there were unofficial regulations within each regiment which suggest how to deploy a skirmish line. General Mikhailovsky-Danielevsky, an aide-de-camp to Alexander I in 1814, writes in *History of the Campaign in France*, 'In the course of their numerous campaigns our troops had acquired singular perfection in skirmishing, and proved the injustice of the charge so often made of their inferiority as marksmen to the sharpshooters of foreign armies.'

Like the skirmishers of other countries, the Russian jägers worked in pairs. The Russians also seem to have adopted the technique of using two skirmish lines towards the end of the Napoleonic Wars because in 1818 General Diebitsch, who was the Russian commander in chief in the 1820s, complained to the Grand Duke Constantine:

The face of battle. Casualty figures are always difficult to calculate, with each side for propaganda reasons overestimating the enemy's casualties while down playing their own. In battles such as Borodino in 1812, 43,000 Russians were killed and wounded compared to between 30,000–40,000, or about a third, of the opposing armies. (Painting by P. H. Hess of the Battle of Borodino, courtesy of the Russian State Museum)

'As to the double chain of skirmishes adopted in the Guard, the C in C [Barclay de Tolly] has not admitted it useful to adopt this rule in the army, having been convinced by the corroborating experience of his service, and even more so in the last war, that in an engagement with the enemy such a chain is not only useless, but it rather leads to unnecessary casualties and confusion; on the contrary, it is well known that a single chain with [a] reserve may be of great use.'

Firing

Paul I's infantry regulations recommended the use of sequence firing by platoons; each platoon would fire separately, the first fired while the second levelled their muskets in the firing position. The third platoon would pull back the hammers on their locks ready to fire, ready to level their muskets once the second platoon had fired. This procedure would be repeated along the line, with the platoons reloading once they had fired. In practice, however, volley fire was used, all the platoons fired at once, the first rank kneeled while the second and third ranks stood while firing.

Firing could be either direct or oblique: 'it is possible to order one division of a battalion or one battalion from the regiment to fire indirectly, to the right or left ... it is possible to slightly turn the division or battalion. Producing this oblique firing can be useful if the enemy attacks in column or on a short frontage. By

'Grenadiers advancing in column', by J. Paul Fischer. The sword belts date this to pre-1808. (The Royal Collection © 2001 Her Majesty Queen Elizabeth II)

oblique firing it is possible to hit him in the flanks. [Also] if he falls on one unit ... then the other units ... are able to ... fire at the attacking unit'.

By 1807 there seems to have been a practice of firing from the hip to obtain the maximum shots per minute. It is not known how widespread this practice was, but the Russian War Ministry discouraged it, not only was it dangerous to the person firing and any comrade on his right, but it was believed that a quarter of the musket balls fired hit the ground.

THE SOLDIER IN BATTLE

The Russian soldier was stubborn in defence and aggressive in attack; all who witnessed the Russians in battle admired their courage, whether friend or foe. Diplomat, and Napoleon's Master of horse, General Armand Caulaincourt, recorded in his memoirs that while on St Helena Napoleon declared, 'These Russians let themselves be killed like automatons; they are not taken alive.' Moreover Wellington wrote on 14 February 1813, after Alexander I had offered to send him some Russian troops to serve in Spain, 'There can be no doubt that this number [15,000] of troops (of Russians particularly) would have the most decisive effect on the next campaign. Even if 1,000 or 2,000 only were sent it would show the power of the Russian Empire.'

Like other nationalities, the Russians were 'fortified by copious distributions of alcohol', to numb their nerves to what was to come.

The Satschen Ponds, at Austerlitz, where according to French propaganda 20,000 Russians drowned while trying to escape over the frozen lakes. However, the exact figure will never be known: a letter in the Austrian Archives states that just two or three bodies were found in the lakes and they had died from wounds rather than from drowning.

Baron de Marbot, a Frenchman who served with Napoleon's Grande Armée, recalls at the Battle of Eylau that the Russian infantry were 'soaked with spirits'.

Usually battles began with an artillery duel, but unlike other nations – who tried to protect their men from artillery – the Russians took no such precaution, which resulted in regiments taking heavy casualties even before they had fired a shot.

Nadezhda Durova, who dressed as a man so that she might serve her country, gives a dramatic version of an advance in her memoirs:

> 'Their bayonets glitter, and the drum is heard ... [and then] comes our fine, disciplined, menacing infantry and the main defence, the powerful bulwark of our native land, the invincible musketeers! ... every time I watch the infantry advancing at a sure, firm pace, with fixed bayonets and menacing drum roll, I feel an emotion which has something both of reverence and dread, I don't know how to express it ... when the columns of infantry rush toward the enemy with their rapid, smooth, disciplined motion, there are no more gallant lads, that's all over: these are heroes who bear inevitable death or go to inevitable death themselves, there is no middle ground ... the infantry formation is death itself, dreadful, inevitable death.'

As the two opponents came closer to one another, they would fire at each other and if one side did not break they would fall on the enemy with the bayonet.

For battle Russian General Suvarrov recommended:

> 'Fire seldom, but fire sure! Push hard with the bayonet! The *ball* will lose its way the *bayonet* never! The *ball* is a fool, the *bayonet* a hero! ... Be sure your ball's in your gun! If three attack you, stab the first, fire on the second and bayonet the third! This seldom

The aftermath of battle. Following the Battle of Zurich in 1799, C. Masson recorded that 'there was hardly one of the mortally wounded Russians who had not clutched at the image of the patron saint which he wore about his neck, and pressed it to his lips before drawing his last breath'. (Courtesy of the Russian State Museum)

happens. In the attack there's no time to load again. When you fire, take aim at their guts; and fire about 20 balls'.

Despite Suvarrov's recommending the bayonet, firefights were more common than hand-to-hand fighting. However, the private soldier preferred to use the bayonet; not only was he armed with an inferior quality musket than his opponents, but also had to buy the lead to make musket balls (for which he was provided with munitions money). Coupled to this, Russian gunpowder was of a very poor quality. Bayonet charges did take place, as detailed by a French source: 'Their method is to charge the enemy with the bayonet, at full speed, crying "*Oorah, oorah*", no troops in the world can stand his charge, the firing does not abate their impetuosity, they attack a battery in front, if that is a readier way, than to attack it in the flank.'

The French General Thiebault observed the hand-to-hand fighting at the Battle of Austerlitz:

With the practice of giving false musters rife in the Russian army, exact casualty figures are hard to calculate. This chart shows the number of men within a division before and after the Battle of Borodino.

Regiments	Mustered before the battle			Casualties						Mustered after the battle		
					killed		wounded		missing			
Grenadier Division	NCOs	Privates	Total	NCOs	ORs	NCOs	ORs	NCOs	ORs	NCOs	ORs	Total
Kiev Grenadiers	47	878	925	5	152	20	338	3	92	19	388	407
Moscow Grenadiers	50	969	1019	6	99	23	430	5	80	16	350	366
Astrahan Grenadiers	58	679	737	8	167	16	522	0	61	34	229	263
Fangorin Grenadiers	50	907	957	9	75	22	47	4	236	15	449	464
Siberian Grenadiers	56	750	806	6	157	11	103	5	196	34	294	328
Little Russia Grenadiers	51	641	692	10	48	17	149	6	200	18	244	262
	312	4824	5136	44	698	109	1589	23	865	136	1954	2090

Regiments	Mustered before the battle			Casualties						Mustered after the battle		
					killed		wounded		missing			
27th Infantry Division	NCOs	Privates	Total	NCOs	ORs	NCOs	ORs	NCOs	ORs	NCOs	ORs	Total
Odessa Infantry Regt	39	611	650	6	53	22	182	5	231	6	145	151
Tarnopol Infantry Regt	46	677	723	0	79	24	199	2	242	20	157	177
Vilensk Infantry Regt	47	1009	1056	23	372	19	301	0	155	5	181	186
Simbirsk Infantry Regt	43	900	943	13	278	14	252	9	126	7	244	251
49th Jäger Regt.	29	609	638	0	43	11	91	5	89	13	386	399
50th Jäger Regt	34	665	699	2	158	12	177	11	126	9	204	213
	238	4471	4709	44	983	102	1202	32	969	60	1317	1377

Russian prisoners of war in 1812. After the Battle of Austerlitz, the French General Vandamme remarked on seeing some Russian prisoners of the Imperial Guard, 'let those fellows go and they will be in Paris in six years'. Vandamme was just four years out. (Author's collection)

'The Russians had to be beaten down man by man. I saw individuals defending themselves as confidently as if they had been in the midst of their battalions. I noticed others, ready to collapse from multiple wounds, loading their muskets as coolly as on the drill square.'

On the other hand, during the Battle of Austerlitz, Kutuzov reported that 'two battalions of the Novgorod Musketeers ran away without offering the slightest resistance, which spread panic among the whole column'. If this was not bad enough, to make matters worse they did it under Alexander I's nose: he ordered that the privates serve an extra five years in the army and the officers of the regiment were to wear their swords without sword knots as a mark of their disgrace. This humiliation was carried by the regiment for 40 years.

The British Ambassador to Russia, Sir Arthur Paget, was more critical of the Russians whom he described as:

'Brave enough in combat, but their gallantry goes for nothing because they do not know how to direct it or use it to strike home. They charge with the bayonet … but they are so clumsy that they never manage to catch anyone.'

A soldier of the French 4th Light infantry would agree with Paget, because when attacked at the Battle of Krems on 11 November 1805, he wrote; 'The Russians were superior in number but they were encumbered by the size of their greatcoats. Their slow movements gave us a great advantage, and we owed our initial success to the clumsiness of the enemy and our own speed in the attack.'

While the Russian soldier was brave enough in formation, once he was separated from his comrades or the formation disorganised, he was at a loss to know what to do next. Sometimes the soldiers could be rallied, as

at Austerlitz when Prince Wolkonski of Kamenski's brigade grabbed a colour of the Fanagoria Grenadier regiment and three times led the brigade in a counter-attack on the right flank of the enemy. If they were not rallied the soldiers would flee the field like a disordered mob.

In *War and Peace* Leo Tolstoy, (probably recalling his own experiences during the Crimean War) notes the psychological effects of battle, when on the eve of the Battle of Borodino Prince Andrei says:

ABOVE **St Nicholas church, Great Yarmouth, England. Here 200 Russian soldiers from the Helder expedition are buried. Several were buried in the cemetery of Haslar Hospital near Portsmouth, as well as other coastal ports. (Author's collection)**

'Why did we lose the Battle of Austerlitz? Our losses were almost equalled by the French losses; but we said to ourselves very early in the day that we were losing the battle, and we lost it. And we said so because we had nothing to fight for then; we wanted to get out of fighting as quickly as we could. "We are defeated so let us run!" and we did run. If we had not said that till evening, God knows what might not have happened. But tomorrow we shan't say that.'

RIGHT **Table showing the strength of the 7th Infantry Corps that was commanded by General Rayevski at Borodino, after receiving recruits and members of the Moscow Opolochenie on 10 October 1812. Quoted from L. G. Beskrovny's *National Militia in the Patriotic War 1812* (Moscow, 1962).**

7th Infantry Corps	Veterans	Opolchenie	Recruits	Total
12th Infantry Division				
Smolensk	192	247	413	852
Narva	410	251	309	970
Aleksapol	342	237	301	880
New Ingmanland	309	243	296	848
6th Jägers	477	292	383	1152
26th Division				
Nizhegorod	340	209	412	961
Ladogsk	469	240	297	1006
Poltav	328	131	440	899
Orlovski	285	305	405	995
5th Jägers	563	348	381	1292
Total	3715	2503	3637	9855

Certainly the Russian soldiers did not think of defeat at Borodino; in his memoirs Russian General Michael Worontsov recalls his division's conduct – they had been given the honour of defending the earthworks known as the *fleches* on the Russians' left wing.

'On the 26th [August, OS] early began the battle or rather the butchery of Borodino. The whole of the French force was directed against our left flank, consequently on the fleches (defended by

53

This drawing of a casualty from the Battle of Waterloo shows a gunshot fracture of the skull. ' On the fifth day after the battle the soldier was insensible. A portion of the frontal bone, an inch in diameter, was found driven into the brain, and it stood perpendicularly; not possible to extract it, from it being firmly wedged. Trepanning performed ... On removal of the bone a quantity of blood and brain came out, and coagulum was scooped out from betwixt the skull and dura mater.' Despite appearing to improve he died six days after the operation. (Courtesy of the Trustees of the AMS Museum)

my division); more than a hundred pieces of artillery played some time upon us, and the greatest part of the best French infantry, under Marshals Davoust and Ney, marched straight upon us. Our fleches were stormed after a stout resistance, were retaken by us, stormed again by the French, retaken once more, and were at last soon lost again, from the overpowering force employed against us … My brave division was entirely destroyed, and out of 5,000 men, not more than about 300, with one field officer … remained untouched or slightly wounded; four or five of our divisions met with very nearly the same fate on the same ground.'

Lieutenant Colonel Lowenstern who was attached to Kutuzov's staff in 1812, recorded in his memoirs, 'In the heat of battle the Russian soldier kills his men without fear or compunction, but once his opponent has surrendered I have more than once seen the Russian share his bread and his brandy with the enemy he would unhesitatingly have killed a moment before.'

Casualties

Each regiment had a chief field surgeon, two field surgeons, a regimental doctor plus a doctor for each battalion to deal with casualties. They were assisted by 12 hospital attendants and a hospital supervisor. The 12 barbers attached to the regiment could also help out. These personnel awaited the influx of wounded at field hospitals or, as Lieutenant Hunt of the 7th Light Dragoons saw at the Battle of Bergen on 19 September 1799:

This poor victim had his arm shattered from the elbow to the shoulder joint. As if this was not enough he caught tetanus, but survived. (Courtesy of the Trustees of the AMS Museum)

'[They] examine and dress the wounded … these men had each a bundle of linen, some lint and a canteen of water; any object which they examined and considered incurable they left to his fate, and went on in dressing the wounds of those whose cases appeared more

54

favourable. After binding up the part, which was done with much expedition, they gave the man a drink of water and proceeded in their duty'.

Usually the wounded were left on the battlefield until they either died or were found and taken to hospital. For the majority the former was their fate. Colonel Lubin Griois who was with the Grande Armée at Borodino, recorded that the Russian wounded;

'overcome by their sufferings and by the cold of the night, made no complaint. Indifferently they watched the passing troops, and tried as far as possible to avoid being kicked by the horses. This insensibility, which I believe stems from a stronger and less sensitive make-up than our own, was increased still further by their fervent devotion to their great St Nicholas. Nearly every wounded soldier clasped a medallion or image of the Saint which they kissed eagerly and which helped them forget their pain'.

Those who were wounded in battle were said to have crawled eastwards, so that they could be nearer to their homeland when they died. The lucky made it to a makeshift hospital either by wagon or under their own steam. Sir Robert Wilson recalls, 'After the Battle of Eylau the wounded Russians and French at Konigsberg, did experience the kindest treatment, and 10,000 men in the hospitals were regularly dressed.' The Prussian General, Count Gneisenau, Blucher's chief of staff, was surprised to see how happy the patients were in these hospitals. There were never enough hospitals to dress all the casualties.

Among the wounded of the Battle of Leipzig was Pamfil Nazarov who was shot in the right leg above the knee, several other musket balls hit his greatcoat, but caused no injury. After a protracted journey, including a night in the open, Pamfil was joined by two other wounded soldiers. They reached a village: 'in which we spent the night, and my leg was so swollen that it was impossible even to remove my boot, which I was forced to cut to release the leg ... [we] continued on the journey for several days to the appointed hospital and my wound more and more became infected'.

Pamfil's group arrived at Pleven in Saxony, where they were given quarters by the churchyard, the church already housing about 400 wounded:

'I laid until 28 October ... In the morning I was given two crutches on which I was able to walk ... The parish physician bandaged our wounds and observed my wound was already completely gangrenous, because it had not been dressed for 13 days.'

Those who survived their wounds but who were no longer fit for active service might receive a pension, like Private Ivanov of the 24th Jäger Regiment who received 25 roubles for having his right arm blown off at the Battle of Kalish and was transferred to the Kamishevskoi District's Serving Invalids. Invalid companies were attached to garrison battalions, which policed the area they were stationed in.

PARADES

There were two types of parade: ceremonial and the victory parade. Although ceremonial parades were common during Catherine the Great's day, the officers were lax about attending and up to a third of the regiment were absent, performing some duty or work for its colonel. Upon Paul I's accession he introduced early morning parades, whatever the weather, which all had to attend. During these *Wachtparad* (or Watch Parades) Paul I would sentence soldiers to be flogged and reduce officers and NCOs to the ranks. On one occasion Paul I ordered a regiment to march 'straight ahead! To Siberia, march!' after it made a mistake. Fortunately for the regiment the Tsar changed his mind.

'The Allies' entry into Paris', in 1814 by an unknown artist. Pamfil Nazarov took part in this parade and wrote that 'several thousand people shouted "Hurrah Alexander! Hurrah the Russian forces!" ' (Author's collection)

A parade in St Petersburg, c.1805. Parades were a popular pastime for both Paul I and Alexander I, who used any excuse to hold them. (Courtesy of the National Army Museum)

While still Tsarivich, Alexander I wrote to his tutor La Harpe complaining, 'The army wastes almost all its time on the parade ground.' If the officers and the men thought that the parades would stop once Paul I had been assassinated, they were disappointed; Alexander I, also loved them and did not miss an opportunity to have a parade. General Muraviev-Karsky records that three parades were held after the Battle of Teplitz in October 1813 during which he could smell the dead bodies that remained unburied.

Pamfil Nazarov was also present at the victory parades at Teplitz in October 1813: 'in the morning being given orders that all the Guards corps were to parade for a thanksgiving service … [since the parade was to be] in the presence of the Sovereign … this town having warm water … the Sovereign paid not a little amount of money so that the Guards' corps was able to wash without prohibition'.

Unfortunately for the Guards corps, later that day they were ordered to bury the bodies of the enemy that Muraviev-Karsky had smelt.

Sometimes these parades had beneficial effects: if the Emperor was pleased with their performance he would reward them financially with a contribution to their *artel* fund.

While the allies were in Paris in 1814 Pamfil records that 'frequent parades, exercises and guard duty' took place. Muraviev-Karsky also confirms this: 'in Paris the soldiers had more work than on campaign as there was so many parades while we were there'.

The biggest parade that was held was at Vertus, near Montmirail, on 10 September 1815, where 150,000 Russian troops marched passed the Duke of Wellington, the Emperors of Russia and Austria and the King of Prussia, all in perfect order. Wellington declared, 'I would never have believed that an army could be brought to such perfection.' The following day a 'Te Deum' was held as a thanksgiving for the allies' victory over Napoleon.

AFTERMATH

Early in 1814 Pamfil Nazarov left hospital and after a few days was ordered to return to his regiment, but was taken ill and admitted to hospital again. He recovered in time to take part in the action at Budissin, before marching on to Paris where on 31 March 1814, just as his regiment was ordered into action, the gates opened and an envoy rode out with the keys to the city and other documents, and announced the city had surrendered. 'The general ordered the commander to receive the keys and packet, giving the sign by taking off his hat and throwing it into the air ... we shouted "oorah!" '

When not on guard duty or taking part in one of the many parades the Russians were confined to their quarters, so that they would not see the freedom other nations had, which might lead to indiscipline. 'Our Emperor', wrote the Russian General Nikita Muraviev, 'gave the Parisian National Guard orders to arrest our soldiers if they met them on the street. This resulted in not a few brawls, in which we generally got the best of it.'

During the second occupation of Paris the Russians were again ordered to remain in their quarters, which prompted Captain Mercer, of the Royal Horse Artillery, to write of the Russian soldier in 1815:

> 'Curiosity they have none, or it is restrained by their discipline, for I do not recollect once having met a Russian soldier dressed and walking the streets, as if to see the place. Sometimes, in passing their quarters, I have heard them sing in their squalling drawling style, in a voice as if mocking someone; there is however something wild and plaintive in their ditties.'

If, against all odds, a soldier completed his 25 years service he would be discharged from the army. He would receive some money from the *artel* fund to help him in civilian life. In theory discharged soldiers returned to their villages where, as freemen rather than serfs, they were kept by the civil authorities. In practice they had no land to support them and so they had to resort to begging.

If he was lucky, an ex-soldier would be transferred to an Invalid Company within a Garrison Battalion where he would find a structured life on half pay. In 1812 de Raymond wrote that the Russian soldier 'generally serves in the army for as long as he can and then joins a garrison, where he performs ordinary service until he becomes an invalid; he is then put in a monastery where, thanks to a frugal diet, he vegetates for a little while longer'. There were a few invalid hospitals for the 'completely incapacitated'. Some did go back to their villages; those that did not had to fend for themselves as best they could until they died.

To Pamfil and his comrades the fall of Paris in 1814 marked the end of the Napoleonic Wars. However, on this day of celebration they were not to know that Napoleon would return from exile the following year, and they would have to march all the way back to Paris again. Nor was it the end of army life for Pamfil: he would not be discharged until January 1836, by which time he would have taught himself to read and write.

MUSEUMS AND COLLECTIONS

Most artifacts are found in museums in Russia, notably in The Hermitage, the Artillery Museum and the Russian State Museum, all in St Petersburg. There is the Borodino Museum at the battle site and the Borodino Panorama in Moscow. In the West, Les Invalides in Paris probably has the largest collection of captured Russian artifacts, including colours and items of uniforms.

OPPOSITE TOP **A portrait of Ivan Galchenko, a Ukrainian who served in the Semenovski Guard Regiment. His greatcoat is adorned with medals for the battles of 1812 and the Kulm cross and his forage cap records that he belongs to the 1st Grenadier Company. His moustache is in the 'uninterrupted' style as was common with grenadiers. (Courtesy of the Borodino Museum)**

OPPOSITE BELOW **Portrait of Ivan Kondratov, who came from the Kursk province and also served in the Semenovski Guard Regiment. He wears the decorations awarded for taking part in the battles of 1812. He also served in the 1st Grenadier Company of the regiment. (Courtesy of the Borodino Museum)**

BELOW **A portrait of Leotinus Shitikov, a former NCO of the Jäger Regiment of the Imperial Guard. He was wounded twice at the Battle of Borodino and took part in the battles of 1813 and 1814. His medals include the cross awarded to those present at the Battle of Kulm and the medal for the Battle of Paris. On his left sleeve he has three yellow strips for 20 years distinctive service. (Courtesy of the Borodino Museum)**

GLOSSARY

Administration
Kazennaya palata Local government officer
Rekrutskoye prisutstviye Recruiting Board
Ukaz Imperial decree
Voyennyy priemschchik Military receiver of recruits
Zapasnyya Rekrutskiya Depo Replacement Recruit Depot

Organisation
Armiya army
Korpus corps
Diviziya division
Brigada brigade
polk regiment
bataillion battalion
rota company
Vzvod platoon
Petota infantry
Starski unter-offizier sergeant
Mladchi unter-offizier corporal
Rotnye barabanshchik company drummer
Polkovyi barabanshchik regimental drummer
Fleishchik fifer
Grenader grenadier
Fuzelernyya fusilier
yeger jäger
Mushketer musketeer
Ryadovoi private
Soldar soldier

Items of uniforms
Kiwer shako
Grenaderskaya shapki grenadier's cap
Treugolnyya tricorn
Kokada cockade
Kisti pompon
Furashka shapki forage cap
Mundir soldier's coat
Fufaika warm coat
Galstuk neck cloth
Pantaloni pantaloons
Shtany trousers
Sapogi boots
Shinel greatcoat
Patronna sumka cartridge box
Perevyaz crossbelt
Portupeya sword belt
Ranetz knapsack
Vodonossnaya flyazha water flask
Shpaga sword
Temlyak sword knot
Ruzhe musket
Shtyk bayonet
Kortik sword bayonet used by jägers
Remen sling

Measurements
1 vershok 4.4 cm
1 arshin 71 cm
1 verst 1.06 km

BIBLIOGRAPHY

Printed primary sources

Complete Collection of the Laws of the Russian Empire (Series 1), 1801–25

Anon, *Russian Archives*, vol. VII, Nikita Mihailov (Moscow, 1996)

General Bagration, *Sbornik Dokumentov i materialov*, Dept. of State and Public Institutions (Moscow, 1945)

Carr, J *A Northern Summer, or travels around the Baltic, through Denmark, Sweden and Russia in the year 1804*, Philip Richards (London, 1805)

Clarke, E *Travels in various countries of Europe vol. 1 Russia*, Cadell & Davies (London, 1810)

Coxe, W *Travels into Poland, Russia, Sweden and Denmark*, S Price (Dublin, 1784)

Kutuvov, M I *Sbornik Dokumentov*, 5 volumes, Ministry of Defence (Moscow, 1950–1956)

Lyall, R *The Character of the Russians*, T Cadell (London, 1823)

Mineav, I M 'Vospominaniia Ivana Menshogo 1806–1849', *Russkaia Starina* (St Petersburg, 1874)

Nazarov, P N 'Zapiskki soldata Pamfilova Nazarova v inochestve mitrofana 1792–1839', *Russkaia Starina* (St Petersburg, 1878)

Porter, R K *Travelling sketches in Russia and Sweden during the years 1805, 1806, 1807 and 1808*, John Stockdale (London, 1809)

Regulations of His Imperial Majesty concerning the service of infantry (St Petersburg, 1798)

RGVIA *Borodino, documents, letters and memoirs*, Imperial Academy of Sciences (Moscow, 1962)

Tugenev, A M 'Notes' *Russkaia Starina 1887* (trans. M Conrad), *Kiwer*, Newsletter of the Russian Army Study Group (1999)

Marchioness of Londonderry (ed.) *The Russian journals of Martha and Catherine Wilmot*, Macmillan & Co. (London, 1934)

Wilson, R *Brief Remarks on the character and composition of the Russian Army*, T. Egerton (London, 1910)

Wilson, R T *A sketch of the military and political power of Russia in the year 1817*, Ridgeway (London, 1817)

Secondary sources

Britten, P A *1812*, 3 vols, Greenhill Books, (London, 1993–96)

Beskrovnyi, L G *The Russian Army and fleet in the 19th century*, Academic International Press, (USA, 1996).

National Militia in the Patriotic War 1812, Imperial Academy of Sciences (Moscow, 1962)

The Patriotic War 1812, TGVIA (Moscow, 1962)

James, A B *1812, Eyewitness accounts of Napoleon's defeat in Russia* Macmillan, (London, 1966)

Europe against Napoleon, The Leipzig campaign 1813 Macmillan, (London, 1970)

Chandler, D *Austerlitz 1805*, Osprey Publishing (Oxford, 1990)

(Editor) *Dictionary of the Napoleonic Wars* Wordsworth Military Library, (Chatham, 1999)

Curtiss, J S *The Russian Army under Nicolas I*, Duke University Press (Durham, NC, 1965)

Duffy, C *Russia's Military Way to the West*, Routledge Kegan & Paul (1982)

Eagles of the Alps, Emperor's Press (Chicago, 1999)

Austerlitz, 1805 Seeley Service & Co. (London, 1977)

Durova, N *The Cavalry Maiden* trans. Mary Flemming Zirin, Paladin (London, 1988)

Falzone, I *L'Esercito Russo 1805/15 Fanteria* De Bello (Milan, 1986)

Hartley, J P *A Social History of the Russian Empire 1650–1825*, Longman (London, 1999)

Haythornthwaite, P *The Russian Army of the Napoleonic Wars (1) Infantry*, Osprey Publishing (Oxford, 1987)

Haythornthwaite, P & Chappel, M *Uniforms of 1812*, Blandford (Poole, 1982)

Josselson, M & Josselson, D *The Commander, A Life of Barclay de Toll*, Oxford University Press (Oxford, 1980)

Keep, J H *Soldiers of the Tsar*, Clarendon (Oxford, 1985)

'Catherine's Veterans', *Slavonic and East European Review*, 59, pp 385–96 (London, 1981)

'The Russian Army's Response to the French Revolution' *Jahrbucher fur Geschichte Osteuropas* (1980) 28, pp 500–523

Leonov, O and Ulyanov, I *Regular Infantry, 1698–1801*, ACT (Moscow, 1995)

Mollo, B & Mollo, J *Uniforms of the Imperial Russian*

Army, Blandford (Poole, 1979)

Olszewski, Z *They will break their teeth on us*, privately published (USA, 2000)

Osipov, K *Alexander Suvarrov*, Hutchinson & Co (London, 1941)

Russian General Staff *The Centenary of the War Ministry* (St Petersburg, 1902–13)

Smith, D *Borodino*, Windrush Press (Gloucester, 1998).

Spring, L 'Life in the Russian infantry' *Age of Napoleon* (1999) no. 29 pp 30-34, Partizan Press (Leigh-on-Sea, 1998)

Stein, F *Geschichte des Russischen Heeres* (Hanover, 1885)

Ulyanov, I *Regular Infantry, 1801–55*, ACT (Moscow, 1997)

Viskovatov, A V *Historical Description of the Clothing and Arms of the Russian Army* 30 volumes, Military Topography Office (St Petersburg, 1851)

Historical Description of the Clothing and Arms of the Russian Army: Organisation of Paul I's army, trans. L Spring, in 'Spring Offensive' (Woking, 2000)

Historical Description of the Clothing and Arms of the Russian Army, volumes 10a and 10b (Organisation 1801–1825) trans. M Conrad, Partizan Press (Leigh-on-Sea, 1993)

Wirtschafter, E K *From Serf to Russian Soldier*, Princeton University Press (Princeton, 1990)

'Military justice and social relations in the pre-reformed army, 1796–1855 *Slavic Review* (1985) vol. 44, University of Illinois (Chicago, 1985)

'The lower Ranks in the peacetime regimental economy of the Russian Army, 1796–1855', *Slavonic and East European Review* (1986,) vol 64, Maney Publishing (London, 1986)

The Triumphal Arch, erected in honour of the Guards' return to St Petersburg in July 1814, by I. A. Ivanov. (Courtesy of the Russian State Museum)

COLOUR PLATE COMMENTARY

A: PRIVATE, MOSCOW GRENADIERS, SMOLENSK INSPECTION, 1805

The central figure shows a grenadier as of 1805, wearing the newly introduced cylindrical shako which has a thick plume (49 cm high and 20 cm in diameter). The collars and cuff are in the inspection colours, which in the case of this figure, are white of the Smolensk inspection. The red shoulder straps denote the senior regiment, the Moscow Grenadiers.

1 Soldier's coat, 1797; this coat was replaced on 30 April 1802 by the one worn by the central figure. 2. Forage cap, 1797. 3. The grenadier's mitre and (4) fusilier's mitre had a different coloured band and back depending on the regiment. They were replaced on 13 February 1805 by the shako (as worn by the central figure). 5. Knapsack from Paul I's reign, made of leather. 6 Knapsack 1802 pattern. 7. Sword belt: it was replaced by a crossbelt on 19 December 1807. 8. A detail of the stitched edging on the sword belt. 9. Cartridge box with a brass plate bearing a Russian double-headed eagle. Grenadiers have a grenade in each corner of the flap. 10. Sword, introduced in 1796: it has a brass handle and was housed in a brown leather scabbard (11). 12. Water flask, of white metal: the stopper doubles as a cup, and this was usually fixed to the knapsack. 13. The 1796 pattern musket was a modified version of the Prussian 1782 pattern musket; the stock was made of walnut and usually painted black. 14. Sword knots: 1st Company white, 2nd red, 3rd sky blue and 4th orange.

B: RECRUITS ARRIVING AT A SUPPLY DEPOT, 1808

In October 1808 Replacement Recruit Depots, each consisting of six companies, were set up. According to Viskovatov, this was 'to avoid the deficiencies connected with the hasty distribution of recruits to regiments after their enlistment'. At first there were only 27, but others were established as the beneficial effects of the depots were realised. However, upon the Grande Armée's invasion of Russia, the depots were disbanded.

Here we see some new recruits arriving at a depot in 1808. These serfs in the foreground are shown in peasant dress, though it was common for new recruits to be issued uniforms at the time of recruitment. In the background to the right, a detachment of recruits practises marching under the watchful eye of an NCO: they are wearing the issued grey recruits' clothing. To the left, two ranks of men stand in dress uniform, whilst in the centre a field officer and a company officer (in the longer coat) are observing proceedings.

The majority of drill movements of the Russian Army were identical to other nations; Russia, as well as Britain and Prussia, looked to Frederick the Great for inspiration when reforming their armies. Following the successes of the French, however, the Russian drill was superseded by a simplified version of the French system.

C: DISCIPLINE AND PUNISHMENT, 1807

This scene depicts 'running the gauntlet', one of the many practices used to punish soldiers. This punishment was not new, nor by any means confined just to Russia. Here the men of the offender's battalion or regiment are shown in undress uniform, and drawn up in two lines facing each other: they are armed with 'fine birch sticks about three feet long'. The unfortunate soldier is marched along between two sergeants who are in full dress. The sergeants are there to prevent him running ahead or turning back. An officer observes the punishment from horseback. If he was lucky the offender would have to walk through just once. John Carr on his tour of Russia in 1804 came across the aftermath of this punishment and noted the sticks were 'steeped in salt brine', which would have further tortured the offender.

D: A COMPANY OF THE NARVA REGIMENT, 12TH DIVISION, ADVANCES INTO BATTLE, 1812

Column formations were adopted by the Russians during the campaigns between 1812 and 1814, mainly because many of the soldiers who had been trained to manoeuvre in line were either no longer alive or unfit to serve. The column formation, which had also become popular with other nations was the only suitable formation that the inadequately trained new recruits could master: it was easier to control and did not need much training to achieve successful manoeuvering. Colonel George Cathcart, ADC to his father who was attached to Imperial Russian headquarters, wrote 'The state of tactical proficiency and discipline of the Russians was in all respects superior to that which prevailed in Napoleon's armies ... They were steady in the ranks and capable of line movements in their campaign of 1806 and appear to have adopted line formations at that time ... [However] in 1812 and 1813, the Russian generals appear to have assimilated their mode of warfare to that of their successful opponent as if they attributed their want of success to a defeat in their own system'.

The infantry column shown consists of sections 23 men wide, and three ranks deep. At the far right of the first rank of men (nearest to the viewer) is the 2nd Lieutenant, who wears a gorget and sash. Behind him on the far right of the third rank, is a Sergeant, distinguished by a quartered pompom on his shako, and with his musket held in his right hand by the trigger guard. The Captain in command (not shown) would march in the middle at the front of the whole company.

E: KUTUZOV REJOINS THE ARMY, 1812

Soldiers from the Pavlov Grenadier Regiment (in their mitres) and the St Petersburg Grenadier Regiment (in shakos) cheer Mikhail Kutuzov on his visit to the 1st Division of III Corps midway through the 1812 campaign. Kutuzov was brought back to overall command of the Russian forces in August

1812 after Napoleon had had the better of the early stages of the campaign. Kutuzov had always been extremely popular with the ordinary soldiers so his return was greeted with rapture. Here the 67-year old acknowledges their cheers, and is accompanied on horseback by General Tutchkov, the Corps commander.

The respect awarded by the common soldiers to Kutuzov did not generally apply to the whole officer class. Although there were enlightened officers who cared about their men (such as General Michael Worontsov, commander of the Russian Army of Occupation in 1815, who set up schools to teach them to read and write) the majority of the officers had no feelings towards their men. Indeed some saw their soldiers merely as a source of income, whether by employing them on a nobleman's estate, stealing from the soldiers' artel fund or even claiming their pay if they were killed.

F: THE BATTLE OF BORODINO, 7 SEPTEMBER 1812

The Battle of Borodino took place on a hot September day. This scene depicts the Russian counter-attack by General Vorontsov's Grenadier brigade of the 27th Division to retake the flèches, one of several earthworks constructed by the Russians to strengthen their line. After an hour of heavy artillery bombardment the earthwork had been stormed by the French General Compans of the 5th Division. These redoubts were defended by Bagration's Second Western Army, saw some of the heaviest fighting, and changed hands several times during the day. It was not until 1130hrs, that the Russians finally abandoned the flèches, which had become a magnet to thousands of soldiers and so resulted in heavy losses to both sides. Estimates of the losses suffered during the battle by the Russians are put at 44,000, but the official return for Barclay de Tolly's army was 9,036 men killed, 17,989 wounded and 9,981 missing – less than 1,000 were captured. These figures do not include officers. Moreover, since most of the officers of Bagration's army were casualties there was not a return made for his army. Here we see a line of Russian Grenadiers charging with their bayonets raised, and shouting. In the foreground, French Voltigeurs, who skirmished in front of the main French line, rush to fall back.

G: THE CAMP AT TARUNTINO, 1812

The camp of Taruntino, south of Moscow, was where Kutuzov gathered his army while waiting for the Grande Armée to leave Moscow. The regiment arriving to join the soldiers of the Vilna Regiment of the 27th Division is one of the many Opolochenie (or militia) regiments, ordered to be raised in July 1812: the majority of the recruits were conscripts. The militia regiments' organisation is not known for certain, but appears to have consisted of three or four battalions: at first each militiaman was armed with whatever he could find. The St Petersburg Opolochenie marched out to join the army after just five days training. However, what they lacked in preparation they made up for in patriotic enthusiasm. Several units served at the battles of Borodino and Maloyaroslavets, but they were gradually absorbed into the regular army.

According to Carl von Clausewitz, by the end of October 1812 Kutuzov had built up an army of 110,000, but when he entered Wilna in December only 40,000 were left. Sir Robert Wilson put the figure at just 35,000 men: 'the Russian troops' he wrote, 'who were moving through a country devastated by the enemy, suffered nearly as much as they did from want of food, fuel and clothing. The soldier had no additional covering for the night bivouacs on the frozen snow; and to sleep longer than half an hour at a time was probable death'.

H: PRIVATE, MOSCOW GRENADIERS, 1812

The central figure shows a soldier in the uniform of 1812; the coat has a closed red collar, lower than before. In November 1807 the practice of having the collars and cuff in the inspection colour were abolished in favour of red. His red shoulder straps have the letter 'M', signifying the Moscow Grenadiers, and he wears the summer gaiter-trousers.

1. In 1807 the shakos were ordered to have leather tops and V-shaped chevrons on the side to make them sturdier. 2. The shako, commonly known as the kiwer (shown here in cutaway view), was introduced on 1 January 1812, although the 1807 pattern continued to be used for some time. 3. Knapsack with water flask; on 14 July 1808 the cylindrical knapsack was replaced by a rectangular one made of black leather. 4. The 1808 pattern musket shown here was much lighter than the 1796 pattern. 5. The greatcoat was made from undyed, dark or light grey cloth and was the same colour for the whole of the regiment. It had the same colour collar and shoulder straps as the coat. 6. A new design of forage cap was introduced on 23 September 1811, the piping around the top of the cap denoting the battalion. 7. A shako plate fitted under the pompon, awarded 'for distinction'. 8 Grenadier's shako and cartridge box badge. 9. Musketeer's shako and cartridge box badge. 10. Grenadier's cartridge box.

INDEX

FIND OUT MORE ABOUT OSPREY

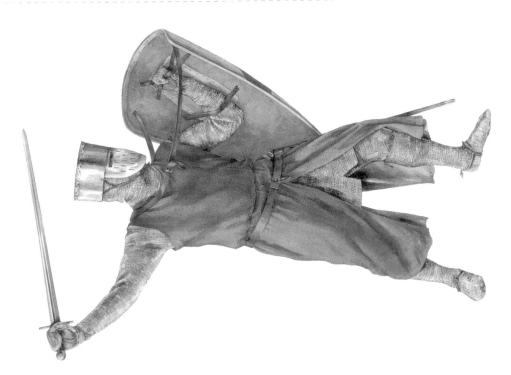

OSPREY
PUBLISHING

www.ospreypublishing.com

call our telephone hotline
for a free information pack

USA & Canada: 1-800-826-6600
UK, Europe and rest of world call:
+44 (0) 1933 443 863

Young Guardsman
Figure taken from *Warrior 22:
Imperial Guardsman 1799–1815*
Published by Osprey
Illustrated by Richard Hook

Knight, c.1190
Figure taken from *Warrior 1: Norman Knight 950 – 1204 AD*
Published by Osprey
Illustrated by Christa Hook

POSTCARD